MW00627781

LIVING & LONGING
FOR THE LORD

Books by Michael Whitworth

The Epic of God

The Derision of Heaven

Esau's Doom

Bethlehem Road

The Pouting Preacher

How to Lose a Kingdom in 400 Years

Splinters of the Cross

LIVING & LONGING FOR THE LORD

A GUIDE TO 1-2 THESSALONIANS

Michael Whitworth

 START2FINISH

© 2014 by Michael Whitworth

All rights reserved. No part of this publication may be reproduced, stored in a retrieval system, or transmitted in any form or by any means without the prior written permission of the author. The only exception is brief quotations in printed reviews.

ISBN-10: 1941972004
ISBN-13: 978-1941972007

Library of Congress Control Number: 2013956164

Published by Start2Finish
Fort Worth, Texas 76244
www.start2finish.org

Printed in the United States of America

Unless otherwise noted, all Scripture quotations are from The Holy Bible, English Standard Version®, copyright © 2001 by Crossway Bibles, a publishing ministry of Good News Publishers. Used by permission. All rights reserved. Scripture quotations marked HCSB are from the Holman Christian Standard Bible®, Copyright © 1999, 2000, 2002, 2003, 2009 by Holman Bible Publishers. Used by permission. Holman Christian Standard Bible®, HCSB®, and Holman CSB® are federally registered trademarks of Holman Bible Publishers. Scripture quotations marked Msg are from THE MESSAGE. Copyright © 1993, 1994, 1995, 1996, 2000, 2001, 2002. Used by permission of NavPress Publishing Group. Scripture quotations marked NASU are from the NEW AMERICAN STANDARD BIBLE®, Copyright © 1960, 1962, 1963, 1971, 1972, 1973, 1975, 1977, 1995 by The Lockman Foundation. Used by permission. Scripture quotations marked NCV are from The Holy Bible: New Century Version®, copyright © 2005 by Thomas Nelson, Inc. Used by permission. Scripture quotations marked NIV are from The Holy Bible, New International Version® NIV® Copyright © 1973, 1978, 1984, 2011 by Biblica, Inc.™ Used by permission. All rights reserved worldwide. Scripture quotations marked NKJV are from the New King James Version. Copyright © 1979, 1980, 1982 by Thomas Nelson, Inc. Used by permission. All rights reserved. Scripture quotations marked NLT are from the Holy Bible, New Living Translation, copyright © 1996, 2004, 2007. Used by permission of Tyndale House Publishers, Inc., Carol Stream, Illinois 60188. All rights reserved. Scripture quotations marked NRSV are from the New Revised Standard Version Bible, copyright © 1989 by the Division of Christian Education of the National Council of the Churches of Christ in the U.S.A., and are used by permission. All rights reserved.

Cover Design: Josh Feit, Evangela.com

To Christians of every tribe, time, and tongue,
who through the ages have anticipated Jesus' return with longing,
who have comforted themselves in their suffering with Paul's words,
and who were sanctified in the meanwhile by the Word of God.

Our wait will not be in vain.

CONTENTS

FOREWORD

The Thessalonian epistles are very important for the church to study because they treat numerous issues that pose challenges for us today. They speak of the need to influence others by our good example (1 Thess 1:7–8), the need for godly, sincere, dedicated leaders (2:1–12), the need to encourage young Christians (3:1–3), the need to live sexually pure lives (4:1–8), the need to anxiously anticipate our deliverance at the Lord's return, instead of being "shaken" from our "composure" and trying to set dates for his return (1 Thess 5:1–11; 2 Thess 2:1–2), the need to teach about God's retributive justice that will come on the disobedient (1:7–9), and the need to exercise loving, yet firm, corrective discipline (3:6–15). These are but a few of the teachings that make these epistles so relevant today.

In *Living & Longing for the Lord*, Michael Whitworth has made a significant contribution to the literature on these two Pauline epistles. Though I would not agree with every single conclusion in this guide, I say without hesitation that it is a well-researched, conservative, and serious treatment of these epistles.

Whitworth writes in an engaging manner, using modern-day illustrations that help the reader to relate Paul's teachings to the problems of daily life in both personal and congregational settings. Several of those illustrations are based on lessons learned from his father, a preacher who passed away while still a young man. Whitworth's guide picks out major topics in the epistles that are needed in today's society and discusses them in an informal, yet interesting, manner.

It is a privilege to recommend this fine work.

— Dr. Earl Edwards
Freed-Hardeman University

INTRODUCTION

It was an unusually cool summer evening in rural Alabama when I obeyed the gospel. Like Paul's jailor in Philippi, mine was a late-night baptism, but in a church camp swimming pool, not the local river. I vividly remember two things from that night. One, I was shivering from the cool night air as I emerged from the water in soaked clothes. Two, I desperately wanted Jesus to return at that moment so that I could experience the glory of the hereafter without the headache of the here-and-now. I didn't want to run the risk of forsaking the Lord, of being a dog that eats its own vomit (cf. 2 Pet 2:20–22). Once a Christian realizes this world holds nothing for him, he longs to be with Jesus. But the perceived delay of Christ's return becomes the breeding ground for Satan's every scheme. Doubts arise: "Why hasn't he come already?" Fears dismay: "I won't be good enough."

How can we successfully live for the Lord while longing for him?

Sometime early in the year A.D. 50, four men arrived at the port metropolis of Thessalonica (population: c. 100,000) on a forgettable Mediterranean afternoon. They entered the provincial capital from the southeast on the Via Egnatia, Rome's magnificent 19-foot-wide highway that connected Europe and Asia Minor. One of the men was a traveling physician, plying his trade from city to city in order to eke out a decent living. The second was a young man in his early twenties, the marks of puberty and adulthood granting him a paradoxical air of exuberance and maturity. The other two men were middle-aged like the doctor, but they bore the distinguishable marks of Jewish ethnicity.

At a passing glance, nothing made these men stand out among the thousands of other visitors to Thessalonica. They appeared road-weary, like so many others, but anyone willing to observe these men longer than a fleeting moment would have noticed something wholly different in their countenance:

A surprising eagerness in the way they moved.

A disarming warmth in how they spoke.

A threatening passion in their eyes.

These were no ordinary men.

This is how I like to imagine Paul and Silas' entrance into Thessalonica, along with their two compatriots, Dr. Luke and the youthful Timothy. They came from Philippi, a city some 60 miles to the east that had given them as much heartache as hallelujahs. There the gospel had found fertile soil in the heart of Lydia and her family, whom Paul's company had met one Saturday on the banks of the Krenides (Acts 16:13–15). But Paul and Silas had also been arrested in Philippi, where they were subsequently beaten and imprisoned illegally. Their bruised backs would have still ached from the beatings, and their thigh muscles would have still quivered from the memory of that midnight earthquake. The apostle did not utter a prayer without giving thanks for the jailor and his family, all of whom had joined the family of God that very night. Paul, however, was disappointed that he had had to leave Philippi so quickly and at the behest of an embarrassed city hall (Acts 16:39).

On the Saturday after his arrival in Thessalonica, Paul attended the synagogue and "reasoned with them from the Scriptures, explaining and proving that it was necessary for the Christ to suffer and to rise from the dead, and saying, 'This Jesus, whom I proclaim to you, is the Christ'" (Acts 17:2–3). Over the course of three weeks, his preaching had a powerful impact on his audience. "Some of them were won over and joined ranks with Paul and Silas, among them a great many God-fearing Greeks and a considerable number of women from the aristocracy" (Acts 17:4 Msg).

Not everyone, however, was pleased with this new rabbi on the block. "The hard-line Jews became furious over the conversions. Mad with jealousy, they rounded up a bunch of brawlers off the streets and soon had an ugly mob terrorizing the city as they hunted down Paul and Silas" (Acts 17:5 Msg). When Paul and his companions could not be located, the mob instead seized Jason, one of the first Thessalonians to obey the gospel, and dragged him before city hall. Their indictment was well reasoned, accusing the Christians of high treason: "They are all defying Caesar's decrees, saying that there is another king, one called Jesus" (Acts 17:7 NIV). As a town known for its staunch support of the Empire and its Emperor, the city fathers panicked and only released Jason when bail was posted. This made it clear that Paul and his friends must leave town. Immediately.

Luke's record goes on to tell of Paul's travels to Berea, Athens, and ultimately Corinth. In each place, Paul again encountered resistance, especially from his fellow Jews. But Corinth proved to be a more permanent stop than previous ones as Paul lingered there for eighteen months (Acts 18:11). Sometime prior, he sent Timothy back to Thessalonica to check on the church because he was eager to learn how his many converts were faring in the aftermath of his abrupt departure. Timothy's youth perhaps made it easier for him to slip in and out of the city while escaping the notice of Paul's enemies. When Timothy returned to Paul with a report on the church's condition, the apostle was overjoyed.

Paul had legitimate reasons to fear the worst. The first-century world was plagued by philosophical and religious conmen. These people roamed from town to town like gypsies, preying on the weak and swindling the rich, only to abandon their "followers" at the first sign of trouble. If the Thessalonians considered Paul no better than these smooth-talking frauds, the church would not have been able to survive his departure. Moreover, Paul's overwhelming success in Thessalonica may have been too much too soon. The converts there had "turned to God from idols to serve the living and true God" (1 Thess 1:9), but were then deprived of the apostles' leadership.

It is hard for us to appreciate the scandal caused by the conversion of early Christians. In the first century, forsaking one's religion wasn't like switching your allegiance to a new sports team. It was, in fact, the ancient equivalent of someone today abandoning modern technology. Imagine a father forbidding his family to own a TV, smartphone, computer, or even a car. His children (not to mention his poor, long-suffering wife) would struggle to relate to almost everyone else—neighbors, classmates, coworkers, etc. They would feel like outsiders in their own community. For the first-century Thessalonians, abandoning the emperor cult to embrace King Jesus put them at severe odds with just about everyone.

What if, however, the Thessalonian Christians had experienced no persecution? There remained many other difficulties that could overwhelm these new Christians. False doctrine, poor leadership, relaxed morals, internal envy, strife, and bitterness—Satan uses all of these to devour the people of God. Imagine, then, the apostle's inexpressible joy when Timothy returned with news that this infant church was not merely surviving, but *thriving*!

It was in this context that Paul penned his first letter to Thessalonica. Timothy couriered the letter to the church, read it, and then returned with their questions and concerns. Second Thessalonians would then have been written just a few months after the first. Collectively, these two epistles explore the practical implications of Jesus' lordship and his imminent return—how we are to go about living and longing for the Lord.

In the church, it would serve us well to recover an eager anticipation of Jesus' imminent return. Theoretically, we know his return could be at any moment, but in so many ways, such a belief has not truly infiltrated our hearts. Our stewardship of time and lack of evangelistic fervor; our certainty of tomorrow's events, an idolatrous dependence on the government, and our overreaction to small slights; the lack of urgency with which we deal with sin—all these betray the fact that we don't really believe the Lord's return could be imminent.

Longing for the Lord, however, will inspire us to live for him, because looking to the heavens exposes what is lacking in our holiness. As we anticipate Jesus' return, our restless hearts find peace in fulfilling God's will for us, even as his Spirit is at work within us. As you read this book and contemplate Paul's letters to Thessalonica, my hope is that life's difficulties will be minimized, Satan's schemes nullified, God's blessings magnified, and his majesty glorified. May you learn what it means to live and long for the Lord. May my prayer become your own, that what begins as but a whisper will flourish into a roar:

"Amen. Come, Lord Jesus!"

THESSALONIANS Q&A

In a recent interview with myself, I asked some questions about this guide to the Thessalonian correspondence. I hope the answers orient you to this guide and to 1–2 Thessalonians.

Q: Who wrote these two letters to the Thessalonians?

A: The apostle Paul. He named himself in the opening of both letters and penned a personal note at the end of one of them (2 Thess 3:17). In the opening verse of each letter, he identifies Silas and Timothy as co-authors, and the pronoun "we" is often used. But Paul is always the dominant speaker throughout. God, of course, is the ultimate author of these letters since his Spirit inspired them (2 Pet 1:21).

Q: When were these letters written?

A: Around the year A.D. 50, and some four to six months after Paul had left Thessalonica. These letters are among the earliest that the apostle wrote, perhaps even the first (it depends on when you date Galatians). From Acts 17–18, we know Paul was forced to leave Thessalonica very quickly. After passing through Berea and Athens, Paul stayed in Corinth for a year and a half. From the Delphi Inscription (a letter written by Claudius Caesar to the city of Delphi), we can date Paul's time in Corinth as ending about A.D. 51, so A.D. 50 seems to be a safe date for the authorship of the Thessalonian correspondence.

Q: Why were these letters written?

A: I explained that in the *Introduction*.

Q: So I should read the *Introduction* if I haven't already?

A: Yes.

Q: If I choose not to read the *Introduction*, what will you do to me?

A: Write mean things about your pet gerbil on Facebook.

Q: Seriously?

A: No.

Q: Where was Thessalonica? What was it like?

A: The city is known as Salonika today. In the first century, it was a Greek
city that served as the capital of the Roman province of Macedonia.
A major Roman highway known as the Via Egnatia ran through the
city from the southeast to the northwest, and it was situated on one
of the best natural harbors in the Aegean. Thessalonica, therefore,
had its fair share of travelers passing through. The church, like the
city, was made up of those representing every walk of life, and this
melting pot led to a few issues that Paul addressed in these letters.
Like many other cities in ancient times, idolatry was deeply rooted in
the social fabric of its citizens. Thessalonica was also a patron city of
the emperor, meaning they took seriously any perceived threat to the
honor and worship of Caesar. Modern readers may easily miss it, but
Paul in these letters spends a lot of time presenting Jesus as a greater
King and Lord than any Roman politician.

Q: Do you have any tips for reading 1–2 Thessalonians?

A: As is the case with all Scripture, we must remember that the literature's genre dictates how we should read, interpret, and apply it. Epistles must be read, interpreted, and applied differently than narrative (e.g. Genesis), poetry (Psalms), or prophecy (Isaiah). A good resource on this subject is *How to Read the Bible for All Its Worth* by Gordon D. Fee and Douglas Stuart.

Q: Can you give an example of how differences in genre matter?

A: First, literary context matters in the epistles more so than in other genres. You don't have to read the other 149 psalms in order to understand the meaning of the 23rd Psalm. It is especially important, in regard to the epistles, to read the whole letter. Attempting to correctly understand and interpret one particular passage cannot be accomplished without knowing the epistle in its entirety. For example, "asleep" in 1 Thess 5:10 doesn't have the same meaning as it does in 5:6, but rather reflects the definition in 4:13. You have to read the entire extended passage to make sense of what Paul is saying. Also, the original audience (i.e. historical context) of the psalms isn't as crucial as it is in other genres. If we were reading a letter written to Thessalonica, Corinth, or Rome, it would help to know something about those cities in the first century. These epistles weren't written in a vacuum.

Q: Were there any surprises in your study of these letters?

A: Actually, yes! I was amazed at how foundational these letters are to the doctrine of Christ's deity. Paul doesn't go into a discussion of the topic in either letter. Rather, he infers and accepts it as truth. You see it in his prayers—whenever he addresses "God," he seems to mean both the Father and the Son (and not necessarily to the exclusion of the Spirit). You see it in his concern for the Thessalonians' persecution—Jesus' deity and lordship was the primary reason for the Christians' afflictions (cf. Acts 17:7). You see it in the apostle's appeals to the OT—he appropriates passages to describe Jesus that were originally about Yahweh. It is impossible to read 1–2 Thessalonians and not feel Paul's unshakeable belief in Christ's deity.

Q: What would be the best way to use this reader's guide?

A: I recommend a four-pass system of reading 1–2 Thessalonians. If you are studying 1 Thess 4:13–18, I suggest reading 1.) all of 1 Thessalonians, 2.) 1 Thess 4:13–18, 3.) that passage's section in this guide (i.e. pp. 86–93), and finally 4.) 1 Thess 4:13–18 again. Reading through the passage several times, plus studying it in this guide, will help cement it in your mind. It might also alert you to something you missed in previous readings.

Q: What can you tell us about how this guide came together?

A: As always, I struggled with what to include vs. exclude. I don't intend for my comments to be exhaustive, and I want to avoid a simple regurgitation of what everyone else has said. I want the reader to understand the Word, so I try to anticipate and answer common questions that arise from the text. Please don't expect me to deal with every issue, just as I don't expect you to always agree with me. Study and reflect on your own and make an informed decision; don't take my word for it. My goal was to present this material in a format that would resemble a friendly, engaging conversation, albeit one-sided. Each chapter ends with a few "Talking Points" that aid in applying the text to life. At the end of the day, I want each person who reads this guide to have a better grasp on what these letters are saying, and, consequently, be closer to God's heart. Ultimately, only the reader can judge for himself whether I have succeeded.

Q: Do you recommend a specific Bible translation?

A: Not really. This guide primarily uses the English Standard Version, but it always helps to read a passage in more than one translation. I'm a huge fan of Study Bibles because of the wealth of information they provide. Just remember that the comments at the bottom of the page, as well as my own remarks, are *not* the inspired and infallible Word of God. Therefore, heed Paul's command: "Examine everything carefully; hold fast to that which is good" (1 Thess 5:21 NASU).

Q: Would you like to add anything else before we conclude?
A: Did you read the *Introduction*?

Q: Yes, and much to the relief of my beloved gerbil!
A: Then I only want to reiterate my hope that your study of 1–2 Thessalonians leaves you excited to live life to the glory of God and more eager for Christ's return. To borrow a phrase from Paul, I pray these words bring you a lot of comfort.

Those who have lived all their lives with Christ
are never unprepared to enter his nearer presence.

WILLIAM BARCLAY

1

WHAT THE LORD HAS DONE

Thanksgiving is my favorite day of the year. I love the intoxicating aromas of dressing in the crockpot, of sweet potato or squash casserole in the oven, of turkey and gravy, orange salad, cranberry sauce, and rolls. I love the joy of family and friends relaxing and enjoying annual traditions: backyard football, board games, the Macy's parade, and holiday films. However, there is so much more to this holiday than food and history; it is also a day set aside to remind us of how truly blessed we are.

You can count me among those grieved over the commercialized encroachment of Christmas on Thanksgiving. It wasn't enough that the day after a national observance of gratitude became known as "Black Friday"—now it has trespassed on Thanksgiving Day itself. Mere hours after giving thanks, millions of Americans line up for a greedy, no-holds-barred free-for-all at big box retailers. I'm quite fond of the popular cartoon that depicts an indignant turkey telling a startled Santa, "This month is for *my* holiday! Now hop in that sleigh and wait your turn!" I think it is important that we have a day like Thanksgiving, because it challenges us to count our blessings, naming them one by one.

The early Christians were all too aware of the importance of giving thanks for God's many gifts. When Timothy and Paul were reunited in Corinth, the apostle was overjoyed to hear the good news about the Thessalonians. It is no surprise that thanksgiving saturates the opening chapter of this letter. Paul knew the Thessalonians had suffered a great deal, but they continued to thrive. Their success was remarkable, especially when we remember that they had none of the things a modern Christian considers so critical to "doing church" (e.g. a church building, organized activities, youth group, seniors ministry). The Thessalonians were simply a group of Christians trying to live out the radical implications of their faith in the midst of a hostile environment. The apostle knew their survival and success were God's work, and Paul knew to thank him for such remarkable grace.

Paul's gratitude at the beginning of the chapter quickly gives way to reminiscence of the Thessalonians' conversion, and, through his words, we are also reminded of our own. We are not entitled to deliverance from God's wrath, for we have done nothing to deserve it. Salvation is God's work, borne out of his deep and abiding love for us. He chose us before the foundation of the world (Eph 1:4), and he desires that we live a life that honors him. The certain transformation God's gospel brings to our lives should be so powerful that we can't help but talk about the change the Lord has wrought. As we contemplate our common hope—Christ's return—we discover that life's dangers, toils, and snares cannot compare to the glory awaiting us on the other side of Jordan. Indeed, our hope is that the same God who so mightily raised Jesus from the dead will work in us until the day of Christ (Phil 1:6). Thus, God's work is our greatest cause for gratitude.

Every year, in the days leading up to Thanksgiving, I contemplate the many blessings I enjoy: a loving wife, an adorable little boy, a multitude of friends who graciously put up with me, a congregation that loves and supports me, parents who raised and nurtured me in the Lord... I could go on and on. The greatest reason, however, for my persistent gratitude is what God has done for me in Christ. I'm grateful for the faith, love, and hope he has fostered in me. I'm grateful for the divine blessing that equips me to live and long for the Lord. As you study the following passage, my prayer is that you also will discover the many reasons you have to be thankful for what the Lord has done.

1 THESSALONIANS 1:1

Like many others, I have often rushed through the introductory comments of a letter, skipping ahead to the more "substantive" parts. It never ceases to amaze me, however, just how much meat exists in something so seemingly inane as a letter's opening. The first verse in 1 Thess 1 identifies the primary author as Paul, but with assistance from Silvanus and Timothy.[1] It is not out of the question that all three had a hand in the composition of both letters to Thessalonica—there are too many "we" passages to ascribe the letters to a single author.

We know quite a bit about Paul, and a little about Timothy. Silvanus, on the other hand, is only mentioned outside the Thessalonian letters in 2 Cor 1:19 and 1 Pet 5:12. In the former passage, Paul says he shared in efforts to evangelize Corinth, and I think we can assume Silvanus made similar contributions in Thessalonica. Who was Silvanus? He was almost certainly the same man whom Luke calls "Silas," the man that accompanied Paul and Timothy in both Thessalonica (Acts 17:1-9) and Corinth (Acts 18:5). "Silas" may have been Silvanus' Aramaic name.

That the church[2] is in both God and Christ (cf. Acts 17:28; Col 3:3) is a heavy concept. First, it is not insignificant that the apostle considers Christ as highly as God. This will not be the last time Paul's high view of Jesus—one that equated him with God—is reflected in these two letters. Second, that the church exists in God and in Christ expresses its radical, otherworldly nature. "Without going even a single line further,

---

1.   In ancient times, it was not customary for an author to name cosenders in the opening of a letter (ZIBBC 3:411), but neither was it unheard of (e.g. Cicero, *To Atticus* 11.5.1).

2.   That this letter is addressed to the church, not to an individual, reminds us that it was meant to be read publicly, a fact Paul will mention in his closing (5:27). Also, he may have chosen "church" over "synagogue" (two words that are essentially synonymous in Greek) to distinguish this group of Christians from the unbelieving Jews in the city (Ben Witherington III, *1 and 2 Thessalonians* [Grand Rapids: Eerdmans, 2006], 49–50). The Greek *ekklēsia* is not exclusive to spiritual use after all, but can refer to an assembly of any kind (cf. Acts 19:32, 39).

we know already that this association, however much it may gather like-minded people, is not in the first instance a social event, a civic club, or a philanthropic organization. It exists only in relationship to 'God the Father and the Lord Jesus Christ.'"[3]

In other words, the church exists primarily to please and praise God. Everything else is a very distant second. The church's power comes from God (Eph 3:20), not from healthy budgets or political posturing. The church's peace comes from God (Phil 4:7), not from civil liberties[4] or overbearing leadership. The church's success comes from God (1 Cor 3:6), not from secular sales methods garnished with evangelistic motives. Most importantly, the church ultimately belongs to no one but God, which means we are subject to his will and plan. It also means we are bound to God's paradigm for the church—not a social network or political organization, but a group of believers seeking to live and long for the Lord together in the midst of a hostile environment.

1 THESSALONIANS 1:2–10

After extending a greeting very characteristic of first-century correspondence, Paul begins his remarks by praising and expressing gratitude for the Thessalonians. Thanksgiving for his readers is a typical feature of all Paul's letter, with the notable exception of Galatians (and for good reason!), and while I do not doubt Paul's sincerity in every letter, he had special reason for giving thanks here. The Thessalonians were new converts to Christianity, little more than children embarking on a new spiritual journey. As a new parent, my baby son's well-being is never far from my mind. Paul's relationship with his converts in Thessalonica

---

3. Beverly Roberts Gaventa, *First and Second Thessalonians* (Louisville: John Knox, 1998), 12. She adds, "Few sermons would confine themselves to a single verse in a letter salutation, yet this one offers an important reminder about who the church is."

4. "The counter-cultural rhetoric in this letter starts right at the beginning. And it is not the emperor who really comes bringing grace and peace, or benefaction and pacification. It is the Father and the Lord," (Witherington, *1 and 2 Thessalonians*, 51).

wasn't that different. He tells them that he "constantly" mentions them in his prayers,[5] giving us a glimpse "of how much Paul lived in an atmosphere of communion with God."[6] They were his children and he their parent, always concerned for their spiritual health.

All of God's servants long for their converts to mature in faith, hope, and love.[7] Paul was prayerful about those things on behalf of the Thessalonians. His choice of words reminds us that faith, hope, and love are not theoretical abstracts, but characteristics to be exhibited through our actions (cf. Jas 2:17; 1 John 3:17–18). The apostle speaks of the Thessalonians' "work produced by faith, your labor prompted by love, and your endurance inspired by hope" (1:3 NIV), what Calvin called "a brief definition of true Christianity."[8]

Faith or trust in God is predicated on what he has done in the past. All of us operate out of faith or fear. A person driven by fear works so as not to get in trouble, but ends up only concerned about appearances and perception. A person driven by faith, however, trusts in what Christ accomplished for us, just as he trusts that the Lord will provide what is lacking in one situation to the next. Notice that Paul is not speaking of works done to merit salvation, but those actions springing from faith. We labor with the (sometimes incomprehensible) belief that God will use our effort as a part of his eternal purpose. If we truly believe God raised Jesus from the dead in his mighty power, we will also believe nothing is impossible for God (Matt 19:26).

Bernard Newman, a veteran of World War I, told of his stay in the home of a Bulgarian peasant. During the stay, the daughter was at work non-stop on sewing a dress. "Don't you ever get tired of that eternal

---

5. "One is left with the impression of regular, persistent, and insistent prayer on behalf of the Thessalonian converts," (Ibid., 56).

6. I. Howard Marshall, *1 and 2 Thessalonians* (Grand Rapids: Eerdmans, 1983), 51.

7. cf. Rom 5:2–5; 1 Cor 13:13; Gal 5:5–6; Eph 1:15; Col 1:4, 23; Phlm 5; Heb 10:22–24; 1 Pet 1:8; 2 Pet 1:5–7.

8. John Calvin, *1, 2 Thessalonians* (Wheaton, IL: Crossway, 1999), 19.

sewing?" Newman asked. "O no!" was the reply. "You see, this is my wedding dress."[9] Like that young woman, some of our work is not just prompted by faith, but also by love. We love our spouses and children, and so we do things for them that we would do for no one else. "Faith works, but *love* goes the extra mile," (Matt 5:41).[10] Paul was grateful that the Thessalonians' love had overflowed in acts of service and sacrifice.

Paul was also grateful for their steadfast endurance in the face of heartache and affliction. The Thessalonians' fortitude was rooted in their common hope—hope that God would keep his promises; hope that the tomb is indeed empty; hope that death was not the end; hope that their King would return and repay the suffering they had endured. Paul speaks elsewhere (Rom 5:3) of how suffering produces endurance, and the Thessalonians had definitely drunk a full cup of affliction. As we will learn throughout these letters, our suffering for the Lord is never wasted or in vain. He redeems our despair and persecution for our good and his glory, using it to make us more like Jesus.

One of the most glorious—yet misunderstood—teachings of Scripture is the election of God's people. What is now a subject of intense debate among Christians was for Paul and the early church a source of tremendous comfort. Although Romans and Ephesians are often thought to be the places where this doctrine is featured most prominently, such a distinction actually belongs to 1–2 Thessalonians.[11] Paul affirmed in 1 Thess 1:4 that the Thessalonians were loved and had been chosen by God (cf. 2 Thess 2:13). Both of these concepts—divine love and election—were reserved almost exclusively for Israel in the OT (e.g. Deut 33:12; Ps 60:5; Isa 44:2; Jer 12:7; Hos 2:23). Here, however, they are applied to Jesus' body, the church.

---

9. William Barclay, *The Letters to the Philippians, Colossians, and Thessalonians*, Rev. ed. (Philadelphia: Westminster Press, 1975), 186.

10. Ronald A. Ward, *Commentary on 1 & 2 Thessalonians* (Waco: Word, 1973), 28.

11. "The language of election is one thing that binds these two letters together and distinguishes them from other Pauline documents," (Witherington, *1 and 2 Thessalonians*, 64).

Paul does not mention their election so as to communicate the impossibility of falling away;[12] why else would he express concern for the Thessalonians' faithfulness in this letter (3:5; 4:1–12; 5:1–11)? No, Paul raises the reality of divine election to affirm God's care and concern for the Thessalonians, and to assure them that God was at work among them as evidenced by their great faith. In the verses that follow, Paul traces the progression of that faith in a unique way.

1. *The gospel came in word, power, the Spirit, and conviction.* Not in word alone—i.e. authentic reception of the gospel is not because of the eloquence or cleverness of the messenger. The gospel is the greatest message the world will ever know, so I'm committed to giving it the best presentation within my capabilities. I know, however, that my oratorical skills are not the deciding factor. There have been plenty of times when I have descended the pulpit with my head held high, thinking I had just preached the sermon of my life, only to be met with a half-hearted "good job" from the congregation. There have been just as many occasions when I felt as if I had let the Lord down with my presentation, only to hear a comment such as, "Thank you for that lesson. I needed to hear that."

The kind of reception Paul had in mind—the kind that produces life-change in the hearer—demands that the message come in word *and* conviction *and* power *and* the Spirit (cf. 1 Cor 2:4–5). The apostle may be affirming that his preaching had been accompanied by miracles performed by the apostles (cf. Acts 14:3, 8–10; Rom 15:19; 2 Cor 12:12; Heb 2:1–4), as well as a miraculous manifestation of the Spirit (i.e. miraculous gifts) among the Thessalonian converts (cf. Acts 10:44–46).[13] Or Paul could have had the non-miraculous in mind, referring instead to the work of

---

12. "Election is conditional upon man's willingness to be chosen and upon his compliance with God's method of choosing. However, even though being chosen is conditional upon the part of man, it always emanates from the great love of God," (Raymond C. Kelcy, *The Letters of Paul to the Thessalonians* [Austin: Sweet, 1968], 28–29; cf. J. W. McGarvey and Philip Y. Pendleton, *Thessalonians, Corinthians, Galatians and Romans* [Cincinnati: Standard Publishing, 1916], 5).

13. The Greek *dynamis*, meaning "power," is used in 1 Cor 12:10, 28–29; 2 Cor 12:12; Gal 3:5; Heb 2:4 in regard to miracles effected by the Spirit.

God's power and Spirit to soften hearts and keep Satan at bay while people hear the message preached (e.g. Acts 16:14). Either way, Paul's preaching had been successful in Thessalonica because of what *the Lord* had done.

2. *A person receives the gospel in the midst of great distress and the joy of the Spirit, thereby imitating early Christians and the Lord.* In direct contradiction to today's Prosperity Gospel advocates (e.g. Creflo Dollar, Joyce Meyer, Joel Osteen), the gospel does not make one happy, healthy, and wealthy. Paul never disguised the Good News in such a way. He was simply grateful the Thessalonians were laboring and enduring. Accepting the gospel had brought trouble upon them, but they had done so because they wanted to serve something alive and true and be saved from God's wrath on the final day. The gospel may or may not make us successful in this life, but it will most certainly make us successful in the one to come! Yet, even in this life, the gospel brings us a mysterious joy that can only originate with God's Spirit (Gal 5:22).

The affliction Paul mentions in 1:6 was not life-and-death persecution, but social harassment. "There is virtually no evidence that Christians anywhere in the Roman empire during the 50s suffered from any organized opposition or physical oppression. Many sources do indicate, however, the offense, even disgust, felt by non-Christian neighbors and fellow citizens when converts to Christianity declined to take part in normal social and cultic activities."[14] This is a far cry from today's church culture. Yes, some converts might be ostracized when they obey the gospel—they're unwelcome at family get-togethers and written out of their parents' will. Just as many, however, are pressured by their

---

14. ZIBBC 3:412. "The exclusivity of the Christians' religion—their seemingly arrogant refusal to participate in or consider valid the worship of any god but their own—deeply wounded public sensibilities and even led to the charge that they were 'atheists.' Christians became easy targets of blame for earthquakes, floods, and agricultural failures, since these and other natural disasters were viewed as punishments from the gods, who felt slighted by this exclusive sect's failure to participate in cultic worship. Family members also felt a strong sense of betrayal over relatives who, on the basis of their newfound faith, broke ancestral traditions and showed an appalling lack of concern for their familial responsibilities," (3:434).

family to become Christians. I've known more than a few parents who became nervous when their child had not been baptized by their mid-teen years. My point is that some of us have no idea the emotional toll exacted on those harassed for their obedience to the Lord.

When I was a very small boy, my family moved to Florence, Alabama. When it comes to the Alabama/Auburn rivalry that consumes the state, my dad quickly learned that the only thing the fans hate worse than their rival is someone who doesn't care about the rivalry at all—i.e. a fence-sitter. It's not much of an overstatement to say that dad felt a lot of social pressure, even among fellow Christians, to pick a favorite team (because dad loved the Lord, he picked the Crimson Tide). Since one team or the other has played for the BCS National Championship the last five years (to say nothing of the epic finish to the 2013 Iron Bowl), the rivalry has hit an unprecedented fever pitch. I imagine the social pressure to choose sides hasn't abated in the least.

This experience, however small, poor, or inadequate it may seem, is in fact a window into the harassment first-century Thessalonians must have endured for turning their backs on community values. I have witnessed the pressure that society can put on someone over a sports team; how much more intense would it have been for the early Christians? Some would have been disowned and shunned by their families, unwelcome at the holiday dinner table. Others would have seen their employment and business opportunities diminished. In a culture where war, famine, and natural disasters were blamed on the displeasure of the gods, the Thessalonians had accepted Christ, forsaking the old ways. Such an offense to established community beliefs would have been met with not a little indignation and fear by their neighbors.

It is more than a little unsettling to consider that the authenticity of our faith is measured by the affliction we endure, but that's exactly what Paul infers (cf. 2 Tim 3:12). The notion that becoming a Christian signals the end of all your problems is completely false; in one sense, problems only begin at that point. Being rejected by friends and family brings sadness, but accepting Christ brings joy and peace that surpasses understanding (cf. 2 Cor 6:10; Phil 4:7). It is through such trials and tribulations, after all, that we imitate our Lord and the early Christians.

3. *Our joy in suffering is a powerful witness to the world.* When the apostle penned this letter, the Thessalonians had not been Christians for very long—six months to a year at most. Paul says, however, that news of their radical conversion, of their joy and endurance in suffering, had reverberated throughout Macedonia (northern Greece) and Achaia (central and southern Greece) like a loud trumpet blast or rolling thunder (cf. Sirach 40:13). They were setting a compelling example for others to follow, and the gospel subsequently "rang out" (HCSB).[15] "They are a model, a flagship church, because they have not only got the truth right, but their faith in that truth is demonstrated in their lifestyle."[16]

Warren Wiersbe cites a survey indicating 70–80% of church growth comes from friendship evangelism.[17] Older methods such as knocking on doors, etc., often aren't as effective as they once were. My dad used to say that no one is at home much during the day anymore—they're either at work or Wal-Mart. On the other hand, consistently being a conduit of the Good News through word and deed has always been, and will always be, the most effective method of evangelism. So potent was the Thessalonians' example and witness that Paul says (somewhat hyperbolically), "We need not say anything" (1:8). That might be another way of saying, "It goes without saying…" when, in fact, we are saying it!

What can't be overstated is the significant reversal in lifestyle the Thessalonians had exhibited. There is absolutely no substitute for actively spreading the gospel through words. Actions and example are not enough on their own, but the more we become like Jesus and less like the world,

---

15. The Greek verb translated "rang out" is *echecheō*; it is used only here in the NT and is the origin of our English *echo*.

16. David Jackman, *The Authentic Church* (Ross-shire, Great Britain: Christian Focus, 1988), 42.

17. Warren W. Wiersbe, *Be Ready* (Wheaton, IL: Victor Books, 1979), 29.

the more attention and glory God's gospel receives (cf. 1:9). Stott calls this "holy gossip"—"the excited transmission from mouth to mouth of the impact which the good news is making on people."[18] We excitedly tell people about new television shows we've discovered, a movie we particularly enjoyed, or the book we couldn't put down. Likewise, the gospel should be so transformative to our hearts that we can't help but share with others how God has transformed our heartache to hope, our pain to peace, our burdens to bliss![19]

4. Receiving the gospel is to embrace God and await Jesus' return. I have always been a bit of a free agent when it comes to my favorite baseball team. Since my childhood was spent in the South, I was an Atlanta Braves fan by default for many years. Then in the late 90s, they lost playoff games with too much of an "Aww, shucks" mentality. I wanted a team that cared, so I started rooting for the Boston Red Sox in 1999, the year Pedro Martinez won the Cy Young award. I was a loyal fan for nearly a decade—until I moved to Texas and began rooting for the Rangers. They have been rather disappointing of late, so I'm currently in the market for a new favorite franchise. I should point out that the Red Sox and Rangers went to a combined four Fall Classics in the time I was a fan, so if any Chicago Cubs fans happen to read this, my support is for hire. Please send a check for $25,000 to...

In Thessalonica, there existed cults dedicated to Serapis, Dionysus, Cabirus, the Roman emperors, and to a lesser extent, Isis, Aphrodite, Demeter, Zeus, and Asclepius.[20] As mentioned in the *Introduction*, for a first-century Thessalonian to turn from idols to the true God of heaven

---

18. John Stott, *The Message of Thessalonians* (Downers Grove, IL: InterVarsity Press, 1991), 38. He later adds that churches should be "like a telecommunications satellite which first receives and then transmits messages. In fact, this is God's simplest plan for world evangelization. If every church had been faithful, the world would long ago have been evangelized," (43–44).

19. "The degree in which the believer is allowed to participate in the sufferings of his Lord, should be the measure of his joy," (J. B. Lightfoot, *Notes on the Epistles of St. Paul* [London: Macmillan, 1895], 14).

20. Robert Jewett, *The Thessalonian Correspondence* (Philadelphia: Fortress, 1986), 126–27.

was a significant decision causing a seismic shift in their relationship to their world. It was from these gods that the Thessalonians had switched their allegiance, deciding "to serve the living and true God."[21] We were not created to be a free people. All of us serve a master, and we cannot serve more than one (Matt 6:24), but how hard we try! Every minister knows the heartache of a recent convert backsliding into his old ways like a dog eating his vomit (2 Pet 2:20–22). Jesus warned that when Satan is evicted from our hearts, we had better usher God in as a replacement and give him our total commitment, lest the devil return even stronger than before (Matt 12:43–45). It's not enough to give up old habits; we must cultivate new ones (2 Cor 5:17); this is why Paul exhorted his readers to become slaves to righteousness (Rom 6:16–23). He was thankful that the Thessalonians had turned from idols *to* God.

Our service to the Lord is not without hope of future reward. After all, we await the return of our King with longing and joy! We are to be more than Christian couch potatoes, marking time until it ends.[22] Serving God faithfully and successfully is only possible with one eye on the work we have to do and the other looking towards the heavens with eager expectation. We live for the Lord because our longing for him has transformed us so completely. Our evangelistic passion, our joy in pain, and our "long obedience in the same direction" (to borrow a phrase from Friedrich Nietzsche and Eugene Peterson) are all solidified by hope in Jesus' imminent return.

Paul closes out 1:10 by invoking the resurrection and the salvation Jesus gives us "from the wrath to come." In so doing, he circles back around

---

21. In the OT, both these terms are commonly applied to God (e.g. Deut 5:26; Josh 3:10; 1 Sam 17:36; 2 Kgs 19:4; 2 Chr 15:3; Ps 42:2; Isa 37:4; Jer 10:10; Dan 6:20; Hos 1:10).

22. "Their waiting was not a mere absence of movement as when one whiles away the hours in meaningless dawdling, but it was an active awaiting directed to the anticipated return of the Lord who was loved and served. As a mother eagerly awaits the return of a son whose coming is more clearly anticipated each day, so the Thessalonians more fully and confidently, with earnest intent, directed their lives so as to prepare for and then participate in the victory of the Lord's return," (William Woodson, *Perfecting Faith* [Brentwood, TN: Penmann Books, 2000], 32–33).

to the faith, love, and hope of the Christian experience—the faith, love, and hope that the Thessalonians exhibited so powerfully as confirmation of the genuineness of their obedience to the gospel. If we truly believe in God's redemptive plan to deliver us from so terrible a fate, then that faith will be coupled with love for him and his people, and a hope that nothing in this world can overwhelm us so long as God is for us (cf. Rom 8:31–39).

God's wrath is fearful and certain, even if it is his "strange work" (Isa 28:21 HCSB). We have all fallen woefully short of his glory (Rom 3:23), but were we ever close to achieving it anyway? "When we display our righteous deeds, they are nothing but filthy rags" compared to God's robes of unapproachable holiness (Isa 64:6 NLT). God's wrath over our sins is righteous and just—it is nothing like the vindictive, capricious anger of a tyrant. We only escape that wrath through his Son (John 14:6; Acts 4:12), a Son whom God sent so that we might be reconciled back to him (2 Cor 5:18–21). "Your idols will not save you," Paul says. "Your political allegiance will not save you. Nothing in all the world will save you from eternal punishment except for what the Lord has done."

Live and long for the King until he comes!

TALKING POINTS

W hat does it mean to turn from idols to God in our time? False gods of wood or stone are no longer in vogue, but that only means that they have been replaced by more abstract forms of idolatry: pleasure and entertainment, tolerance and false love, greed, power, addiction—the list is virtually endless. Our problem is often that we want to be saved from God's wrath with the minimum amount of conversion or "turning" possible. We tell ourselves that we love God, and that there are parts of the Christian life that are tolerable, but we don't want to plunge too deeply into Christianity lest we be ostracized from society. Though separated by 2,000 years of cultural change, one fact remains the same: it is no easier today to resist peer pressure than it was then. The Thessalonians struggled to live and long for the Lord in a hostile context, and so do we. If our Christian experience seems void of "the joy of the Holy Spirit" (1:6), perhaps it is because we have not authentically and completely "turned to God from idols." Either Jesus is Lord of all, or he is Lord not at all.

H ow would your congregation look if everything were made God-centered? I know you'd like to say there would be no change at all, but be honest. How would your worship services be different? Would there be more or less songs? Would the preacher feel free to preach as long as it took to glorify God? Would public prayers sound any different? Would giving increase? What about your church's activities? Would they be oriented around making people happier or holier? Would you ask different questions in order to gauge their effectiveness—"Are we meeting the needs of our members?" vs. "Are we saving the lost and discipling (i.e. disciplining) the saved?" If we want God to be at the center of all things, we must learn to measure growth and success in ways that can't be easily quantified (e.g. attendance, budget, building size). We must also scrap the consumer-mindset that deceives us into wanting something simply because it is new or expensive or wrapped in a pretty package. Since when do any of us have any clue as to what we really want? Only when God is glorified can we be satisfied and whole. This is the secret to successfully living and longing for the Lord until he returns.

R elationships between fellow Christians are special—even holy—things, and we should cherish them. Too often, a minister's labor is oriented around programs or goals instead of people. I am struck by Paul's sincere affection and concern for the Thessalonians; he sought to renew and deepen his friendship with them through writing these letters. Mutual communication has a way of strengthening emotional bonds across long distances. When work demands that I be apart from my wife during the day, phone calls, emails, and text messages go a long way in mitigating the yearning and loneliness. There is still nothing like going to the mailbox and discovering a letter or card from a friend whom we haven't seen in years. In this first letter to the Thessalonians, Paul assures them of his constant prayers (1:2; 2:13; 3:10), his motherly affection (2:7), the pride and joy they give him (2:19–20), and his plans to see them again as soon as possible (2:17; 3:10). How might our relationships be sweeter and more meaningful if we nurtured them with communication as the apostle did?

2

NO GIMMICKS, JUST GOSPEL

I checked my email the other day and received some rather exciting news, both good and bad. The bad news was that a very distant relative, whom I've never met (and honestly didn't even know existed), had passed away. The good news, however, was that as the next-of-kin I stand to receive a rather large sum of the estate. I say "rather large sum" since it equates to something in the seven figures range. I'm still reeling from the excitement of it all, not to mention shocked at how easy it will be to claim my millions!

All I have to do is send a check for $10,000 to Nigeria.

Since 2010, incidents of check kiting and similar fraudulent activities have been on the decline, due mostly to fewer people using checks and an increased use of debit cards (which, of course, has increased debit-card-related crimes). Other forms of financial deceit still exist. Senior citizens are offered help with navigating the red tape of Medicare or Medicaid in exchange for their Social Security number or other sensitive data. Then there is email phishing, which depends on designing an email that appears to come from a legitimate financial institution. Regardless of the form it takes, agents of fraud often prey on a person's inability to know when something is too good to be true. They bait their prey, lure them into the trap, and ensnare them in terrible situations.

Most of us become quickly attuned to such scams, easily sniffing out a deal too good to be true. Whether it is the latest diet fad, check kiting scheme, or a free weekend at a resort in exchange for listening to a time-share sales pitch, swindlers abound at every turn. These crimes are not unique to modern times either. First-century Thessalonica had her fill of charlatans hawking appealing philosophies and the latest feel-good schemes in an effort to profit off/prey on the weak. Their goal was to skip town before their deception was exposed and, to an outsider, this is exactly what Paul and his friends had done. Some believe Paul was responding in this passage to critics outside the church in order to defend his actions and sudden departure. There may be an element of this in his letters, but Paul wrote to assure the Thessalonian Christians of his sincerity.[1] He was less concerned about the opinion of outsiders.

In 1 Thess 2, Paul reminds his readers of his situation when he first arrived in the city, how he had conducted himself while there, and he assured them of his affection and desire to return. He also seems intent on fortifying the Thessalonians against the persecution facing them. The headaches and heartaches of affliction might have prompted some to think that they had backed the wrong horse. Was Paul's message false? Did they forsake one bogus philosophy for another? "Not at all," Paul says. "Your experience is consistent with that of the first Christians."

Paul's response gives us a glimpse into the heart of authentic Christian living and ministry, as well as the true gospel. He sets a powerful example regarding his affection for God's people, his commitment to Christian ethics, his boldness in the face of persecution, and his resolve to please the Lord above all else. Christians would do well to reflect on the apostle's heart as revealed in this passage.

1 THESSALONIANS 2:1–12

To combat any allegations against him, Paul launches into a

---

1. Coffman adamantly contended "that entirely too much has been made of the alleged slanders against Paul," (James Burton Coffman, *Commentary on 1 & 2 Thessalonians, 1 & 2 Timothy, Titus & Philemon* [Austin: Firm Foundation, 1978], 21). He has a point, but I also think that just because the accusations weren't flying doesn't mean Paul had no need to address them.

passionate, yet reasonable defense of his time in Thessalonica. He and
his companions had not been failures there, nor had their message been
exposed as fraudulent—Paul was emphatic about that. "In vain" has to do
with the fruitlessness of an endeavor; "it speaks of the 'zero-ness' of human
words and human endeavors that lack divine content."[2] From this point,
Paul argues that the results of his ministry in Thessalonica, while laboring
against so much opposition, in fact proved the validity of the gospel.

As Luke's record in Acts bears out, Paul's experience in Philippi had
not been entirely positive. He and Silas had been arrested, beaten, and
incarcerated without a trial (Acts 16:22–24). This treatment was illegal
and against the rights of Roman citizens, which both he and Silas were, and
Paul brought this fact to the attention of the city authorities (Acts 16:35–
40). These events had justifiably wounded the apostle emotionally[3] (cf.
Phil 1:30)—even here, he speaks of having "been shamefully treated" (i.e.
insulted[4]), the very same word Jesus used of his own fate (Luke 18:32).

Paul mentions his past experiences in Philippi because it spoke to the
possible allegations made against him in Thessalonica. If the apostle were
just another first-century conman, peddling a philosophy as a part of a get-
rich-quick scheme, why would he continue doing so after being beaten
and imprisoned? The punishment he suffered in Philippi would have been
enough to send a crook out to seek an easier line of work—unless that
person were completely committed to a higher calling such as the gospel
of Christ.[5] But Paul did not run from his work; he persevered. He reminds
his readers that he had boldly declared the gospel in Thessalonica in the

---

2. Philip W. Comfort, "1 & 2 Thessalonians" in *Cornerstone Biblical Commentary*, vol. 16 (Carol Stream, IL: Tyndale House, 2008), 343.

3. "In his insistence on upholding the dignity of Roman citizenship we see something of the deep hurt Paul had experienced in the indignities heaped on him," (Leon Morris, *The First and Second Epistles to the Thessalonians*, Rev. ed. [Grand Rapids: Eerdmans, 1991], 59).

4. BDAG 1022.

5. "Paul and Silas had been beaten and humiliated at Philippi; yet they came to Thessalonica and preached. Most of us would have taken a vacation or found an excuse not to minister," (Wiersbe, *Be Ready*, 36).

face of "much conflict,"[6] reinforcing both his sincerity and devotion.

Religious and philosophical charlatans, driven by greed and pride, infested the ancient world.[7] They roamed from town to town, living off the generosity of their followers, and quickly evacuated when exposed. They weren't that different from the medicine men and snake-oil salesmen of the Wild West. Dio Chrysostom, a first-century orator, described a philosopher who was "being destroyed by popular opinion; for his liver swelled and grew whenever he was praised and shrivelled again when he was censured," (*Orations* 8.33).

If your congregation were searching for a minister, would you hire someone with Paul's rap sheet and employment history? In today's Christian circles, Paul enjoys the "halo effect" of being an esteemed apostle of the Lord, making it difficult for us to really appreciate his concern about being labeled a phony or impotent laborer in the Kingdom.

> There were, no doubt, those in Thessalonica who said that this man Paul had a police record, that he was nothing less than a criminal on the run from justice and that obviously no one should listen to a man like that. A really malicious mind will twist anything into a slander.[8]

The trinity of terms Paul uses in 1 Thess 2:3—"error or impurity or any attempt to deceive"—were common complaints against ancient hucksters. It's no wonder, then, that the apostle spent so much time distancing himself from his secular contemporaries. His mention of deceit especially

---

6. "The word 'conflict' is a vivid one, taken from the vocabulary of athletics, where it meant a contest or a race. It is that from which we derive our word 'agony.' It denotes not a token opposition, a tepid struggle, but a very real battle. It is used of fighting the good fight of faith (1 Tim. 6:12; 2 Tim. 4:7), and that is no half-hearted fight," (Morris, *Thessalonians*, 61).

7. Abraham J. Malherbe, "'Gentle as a Nurse': The Cynic Background to I Thess II," *NovT* 12 (1970): 203–17; Bruce W. Winter, "The Entries and Ethics of Orators and Paul (1 Thessalonians 2:1–12)," *TynBul* 44 (1993): 55–74.

8. Barclay, *Letters*, 188.

resonates with me. "To deceive" or "trick" (NIV) originally meant to bait something, such as fish or game.[9] The term implied that you were using some sort of trickery to lure your prey. One bite of that delicious worm or carrot and BAM! You are caught in the hunter's trap or the fisherman's hook and on your way to becoming dinner. Paul eschewed such gimmicks and any attempt at trickery while engaging in evangelism. He sought only to share the truth, whether it was what his audience wanted to hear or not.

Several months ago, I learned that a nearby church offers door prizes to anyone willing to attend their services. Now, my own congregation gives a loaf of banana bread to visitors on Sunday morning, and while it's delicious, we can hardly be accused of trickery or deception. This other church, however, offers iPods, iPads, and cash prizes to those who visit. I believe in being warm and hospitable to everyone, but this church's behavior reminded me that the only gimmick the Lord's church needs is the gospel itself—the call to bear a cross daily, the summons to come and die.

At the end of the day, Paul knew he didn't answer to anyone but God. He was an ambassador of God's message; he served God, not himself. He rather bluntly explains this point to the Corinthians: "As for myself, I do not care if I am judged by you or by any human court. I do not even judge myself. I know of no wrong I have done, but this does not make me right before the Lord. The Lord is the One who judges me" (1 Cor 4:3–4 NCV; cf. Gal 1:10; Col 3:22). However, knowing that God is our only true Judge is not always a reassuring fact.

> On the one hand, this is a disconcerting fact, because God scrutinizes our hearts and their secrets, and his standards are very high. On the other hand, it is marvellously liberating, since God is a more knowledgeable, impartial and merciful judge than any human being or ecclesiastical court or committee. To be accountable to him is to be

---

9. Morris, *Thessalonians*, 62.

delivered from the tyranny of human criticism.[10]

It is easy for any minister, regardless of his good intentions, to lose sight of so vital a truth. The size of our audience does not matter, nor does the contribution amount, or responses to the invitation, or (in my case) book sales. Each of these things can be gained through deception and trickery. But they don't necessary reflect authentic reception of and obedience to the gospel, and none of it matters if the Lord is not pleased with us.[11]

Paul wanted the Thessalonians to remember how he and his companions had conducted themselves while in town. They were not guilty of flattery, greed, or glory-grabbing. Sadly, ministers driven by greed and glory, rather than a sincere desire to see Christ exalted, have hindered the cause of Christ in the past. Men like Jim Bakker, Jimmy Swaggart, and Robert Tilton may not be recognizable to the new generation, but they did a lot to undermine the good work of others. My dad used to parody televangelists with this mocking motto: "Make your donation for your salvation and my vacation." The comedic singer Ray Stevens even released the single "Would Jesus Wear a Rolex?" in 1987, lampooning a preacher who was "asking me for $20 with $10,000 on his arm."

What Paul is addressing here is not limited to the stigma of televangelism. It lurks in the heart of every minister, and we must remain ever vigilant against its appearance. Living above one's means, telling false stories to illustrate sermons, avoiding "tough topics" or eschewing boldness so as to remain popular or employable—all of these are contrary to the spirit Paul exemplified while in Thessalonica. These actions are, in truth, the very definition of deceit, flattery, and greed described by Paul.

This is not to say Paul did not have the right to demand certain things of the Thessalonians. He was, after all, an apostle and could have

---

10. Stott, *Message of Thessalonians*, 50–51.

11. cf. 1 Sam 16:7; 1 Chr 28:9; 29:17; Pss 7:9; 17:3; 139:23; Prov 17:3; Jer 11:20; 12:3.

easily "thrown his weight around."[12] Instead, he graciously set aside his rights for the greater good of his brethren. Paul says that he and Silas had been "gentle among you."[13] He had the right to be financially supported by the church (1 Cor 9:14), but did not always exercise this right (1 Cor 9:15–18; 2 Cor 11:7–11; 2 Thess 3:7–9) so as not to overburden the Thessalonians (2:9; cf. Neh 5:18; 2 Cor 12:16; 2 Thess 3:8). We know the saints in Philippi sent Paul financial support multiple times during this period (Phil 4:16), but it evidently wasn't enough to make ends meet. There is no record of support coming from Antioch or Jerusalem. It's likely that plied his learned craft of tent-making in Thessalonica, which he later did in Corinth (Acts 18:3). It was customary for all Jewish men to be skilled in a trade to support themselves in their teaching.[14] Paul might have worked from a shop in what was called an *insula*,

> An apartment building with living quarters on the upper floors and artisans' shops on the main floor opening onto the street. Such a location would also afford him access to other artisans and those who frequented the busy center

---

12. D. E. H. Whiteley, *Thessalonians* (London: Oxford Univ. Press, 1969), 42.

13. There is a significant variant here, with some translations reading "gentle" (ESV, HCSB) and others, "infants" (NIV, NLT). In the Greek, the absence/presence of the first letter is the only thing distinguishing the two terms (i.e. *ēpioi* vs. *nēpioi*). "Infants" wouldn't be an entirely inappropriate metaphor since Paul goes on to invoke mothers, fathers, and orphans later in the passage. "Gentle," however, serves as a nice contrast to "burden" (2:9; cf. F. F. Bruce, *1 & 2 Thessalonians* [Dallas: Word, 1982], 31), and Paul never elsewhere calls himself an infant; he actually uses the word in a negative way (e.g. 1 Cor 13:11; Gal 4:3), though not always (1 Cor 14:20). Fee prefers "infants" to "gentle," arguing that it spoke not only to Paul's gentleness, but also his innocence of any wrong-doing (Gordon D. Fee, *The First and Second Letters to the Thessalonians* [Grand Rapids: Eerdmans, 2009], 71). Jeffrey Weima argues for "infants" over "gentle" ("'But We Became Infants Among You': The Case for NHΠIOI in 1 Thess 2.7," *NTS* 46 [2002]: 547–64). But Metzger concludes, "Despite the weight of external evidence, only ἤπιοι seems to suit the context," (Bruce M. Metzger, *A Textual Commentary on the Greek New Testament*, 2nd ed. [Stuttgart: German Bible Society, 1994], 562).

14. "Rabban Gamaliel, son of R. Judah the Patriarch, says, 'Fitting is learning in Torah along with a craft, for the labor put into the two of them makes one forget sin. And all learning of Torah which is not joined with labor is destined to be null and cause sin,'" (*Abot* 2:2).

of the pre-industrial city, and it would be a suitable venue
in which to share the good news.[15]

Instead of living off the Christians' generosity, Paul and his
companions worked their "fingers to the bone, up half the night,
moonlighting so you wouldn't have the burden of supporting us while we
proclaimed God's Message to you" (2:9 Msg).

Paul likened his gentleness to "a nursing mother taking care of her own
children" (2:7; cf. Num 11:12; Gal 4:19). He brought up the metaphor of
a mother's gentleness and love since it contradicted the allegations against
him.[16] In July 2002, Dan Baber put up for auction on eBay an item he
called "Best Mom in the World." The listing stipulated that the winner
would receive an email from his very own mom, Sue Hamilton, promised
to "make you feel like you are the most special person on the earth." The
auction received almost 43,000 views, 92 bids, and the winning bid was
$610.[17] This is the value placed on a single warm, motherly email!

The apostle perpetuates the motherly-metaphor by saying he was
"affectionately desirous of you." This phrase is translated from a Greek word
used on a fourth-century tombstone where it describes parents' longing
for their deceased child.[18] It is possible that the term was also used in the
nursery between mother and child. "If so, we have a further indication of
the warmth and sensitivity of Paul."[19] It would take little imagination to see
how the apostle would have regarded today's ministers who keep it "strictly
professional." He not only loved to share the gospel with the Thessalonians,

15. David A. deSilva, *An Introduction to the New Testament* (Downers Grove, IL: InterVarsity
Press, 2004), 529; cf. Ronald F. Hock, "The Workshop as a Social Setting for Paul's Missionary
Preaching," *CBQ* 41 (1979): 438–50.

16. As Calvin pointed out, a nursing mother cares little about her child acknowledging
her dignity and authority (*1, 2 Thessalonians*, 28).

17. "A Mother's Touch," *Focus on the Family Citizen* (July 2002).

18. ZIBBC 3:415.

19. Gary W. Demarest, *1, 2 Thessalonians, 1, 2 Timothy, Titus* (Waco: Word, 1984), 58; cf.
Marshall, *1 and 2 Thessalonians*, 71.

but also enjoyed being among them. "We were ready to share with you …
our own selves, because you had become very dear to us."[20]

After employing the image of a mother, Paul also invokes that of a father
(2:11). It is often noted that the maternal image reflects Paul's concern for
the Thessalonians, while the paternal metaphor pertains to his instructing
them. "When they failed he encouraged them to try again, and warned
them of the danger of turning aside as a father does his own children."[21]

Like a father, Paul says he and his companions had exhorted,
encouraged, and charged the Thessalonians to live a life worthy of God and
his calling (cf. Eph 4:1). Paul specifically reminds his readers that they have
been called into God's kingdom and glory. Each of us has been invited to
live under God's rule and authority, and to do so to the glory of God. Living
for the Lord is not only for our benefit (e.g. deliverance from hell); we were
created primarily to glorify God with our lives. Our existence is a restless
one until we start fulfilling that purpose. The apostle thus encouraged the
Thessalonians towards "holy and righteous and blameless" conduct so that
God would thereby be glorified as Lord and King.

In March 2013, God blessed my wife and I with an awesome baby
boy. Since his birth, I have come to greatly appreciate Paul's metaphor. My
son was born with a few problems to which I've had a hard time adjusting.
He cries a lot if you don't hold him. He didn't come potty-trained (I blame
that on his being born 18 days premature). At ten months old, he's only
now learning to feed himself, and he gives me a blank stare when I ask
him if he's done his chores. My wife, on the other hand, has this innate
knowledge of what he needs and when he needs it. She is gentle, sensitive,
and significantly less flustered than I. She shifts her daily plans to what is
best for him, totally forgetting her own needs until he is settled. She finds

---

20. Bruce best explains this statement: "We were willing to give ourselves to you, to put
ourselves at your disposal, without reservation," (*1 & 2 Thessalonians*, 32).

21. David Lipscomb, *A Commentary on the New Testament Epistles*, vol. 5, ed. J. W.
Shepherd, (Nashville: Gospel Advocate, 1983), 29. Shepherd adds, "It is the part of a worker in
the Lord's vineyard not to be harsh, censorious, despondent, but fatherlike …"

joy in feeding, changing, clothing, and holding him.

And she doesn't make him do chores. Yet.

Sara's way with our son has inspired me to reevaluate how I interact with God's people. Am I gentle? Patient? Do I celebrate victories, or do I chastise them for what they haven't already achieved?[22] Do I make unreasonable demands of them? These are legitimate questions every minister should contemplate from time to time.[23]

1 THESSALONIANS 2:13-16

Paul knew that the Thessalonians had sincerely received the gospel as an authentic message from God, not men.[24] He knew the gospel was producing its intended fruit in their lives.[25] The proof of this was manifested in the suffering of the Thessalonians, whose experience was the same as the church in Palestine. Luke's record in Acts records how the infant church was persecuted heavily, yet continued to grow in spite of this affliction (Acts 8:1–4), a reality Paul knew all too well, having been on the wrong end of things (Acts 9;1; Gal 1:22–23; 1 Tim 1:13). The apostle wanted the Thessalonians to know that their suffering was not evidence that they had done something wrong, but that their situation was no different than that of all true Christians since the beginning.

---

22. Coffman adds, "He is a poor preacher who neglects to encourage the Christians who hear him. Nothing is more soul-killing and church-diminishing than a preacher who never has any remarks of praise and encouragement for his hearers," (*Commentary*, 28).

23. "Some Christian leaders become both self-centred and autocratic. The more their authority is challenged, the more they assert it. We all need to cultivate more, in our pastoral ministry, of the gentleness, love and self-sacrifice of a mother," (Stott, *Message of Thessalonians*, 52).

24. That biblical preaching comes from God, not man, should make Christians think twice before dismissing a preacher's words. It should also make preachers think twice before relegating sermon preparation to a back burner.

25. "This message was not a philosophical discourse on the means to the virtuous life (or a self-help seminar on how to overcome personal and social issues, as the gospel is frequently portrayed in our era). It was the *word of God*, which powerfully transformed their lives," (Green, *Thessalonians*, 141).

When Christians suffer, they are identified with Jesus and their spiritual ancestors (cf. Heb 12:2; Acts 5:41). In the NT, "Persecution for the sake of Christ is treated as evidence of the genuineness of the faith of those who suffer it."[26] Jesus warned his disciples of its certainty (John 16:33; cf. 1 Pet 4:12), and Paul taught that we cannot enter the Kingdom without it (Acts 14:22). The early church considered persecution to be a badge of honor (Acts 5:41)—sometimes I wonder if the American church considers persecution to be anything but honor. What if we have been misguided in thanking God for our religious freedoms, especially when Jesus said persecution makes us "blessed" (Matt 5:10–12)? I realize how absurd this may seem to some of you. Religious freedom is a bad thing? I might as well call John Wayne or Chuck Norris a sissy. But anyone who views life through the lenses of Scripture must concede that persecution was an identifying mark of the early church, one that the modern church has been quite reluctant to adopt.

In 2:15–16, Paul[27] lays heavy charges at the feet of the Jews (both in Palestine and abroad).[28] These two verses have drawn considerable attention through the years, and especially in recent times, because of the strong anti-Semitic undertone to Paul's words.

> These two verses, sometimes called "the Pauline polemic against the Jews", have been described as "violent", "vehement", "vindictive", "passionate", "intemperate", "bitter" and "harsh". So incongruous do some commentators feel them to be in one of Paul's letters, that they attribute

---

26. Bruce, *1 & 2 Thessalonians*, 50. He goes on (50–51) to point out that the Thessalonians' affliction may have lasted more than six years, that their "extreme poverty" (2 Cor 8:2) may have been the result of mob violence and looting (cf. Heb 10:32–34).

27. Comfort puts forth the intriguing theory that Silas, not Paul, wrote this portion of the letter ("1 & 2 Thessalonians," 347–48).

28. "This section is undoubtedly the most explicit condemnation of any people to be found in all of Paul's writings," (Earl D. Edwards, *1 & 2 Thessalonians* [Searcy, AR: Resource Publications, 2008], 60).

them to an anti-Jewish interpolator. But there is no manuscript evidence that they were added by a later hand.[29]

Stott is right that there is no manuscript evidence to support the theory[30] that these words were added without Paul's knowledge (i.e. without divine approval). Equally ridiculous, however, is to accuse Paul of anti-Semitism, since he was a Jew himself (as were Jesus and the other apostles). A careful reading of the text demonstrates that he is not prejudiced against all Jews (cf. Rom 9:2–3), but is rather frustrated with anyone who rebels against God—Jews, Gentiles (Rom 1:18), or even Jewish Christians (2 Cor 11:3–4; Gal 5:11–12; Phil 3:2)—and who causes trouble for God's people.[31] Furthermore, Paul would later speak of a time when the Jews would be grafted back into God's tree (Rom 11:17–24), which does not suggest that Paul, a Jew, had anti-Semitic leanings.

Nonetheless, Paul held the Jews responsible for the murder of Jesus and the prophets. For many centuries, the wicked and rebellious element in Israel had harassed God's spokesmen whenever they brought words of warning and repentance (e.g. 1 Kgs 19:9–18; 2 Chr 36:15–16; Neh 9:26; Jer 2:30). "Name one prophet your ancestors didn't persecute!" Stephen asked incredulously, and only minutes before his own death (Acts 7:52 NLT). Whenever Jesus' enemies sought to silence him, the Lord would remind his audience that he would be but the latest in a long line of martyred messengers (cf. Matt 23:29–37; Luke 4:24; 11:47–51; 13:33–34). It was the consistent testimony of the early church that the Jewish authorities were

---

29. Stott, *Message of Thessalonians*, 55; cf. G. E. Okeke, "1 Thessalonians 2.13–16: The Fate of the Unbelieving Jews," *NTS* 27 (1981): 127–36; Jon A. Weatherly, "The Authenticity of 1 Thessalonians 2.13–16: Additional Evidence," *JSNT* 42 (1991): 79–98.

30. Birger A. Pearson, "1 Thessalonians 2:13–16: A Deutero-Pauline Interpolation," *HTR* 64 (1971): 79–94.

31. "Just as the Gospel of John uses the term 'the Jews' to designate the Pharisaic-Sadducean leadership that opposed Jesus, so Paul has in mind those Jews who opposed his mission," (Walter C. Kaiser, Jr., *Hard Sayings of the Bible* [Downers Grove, IL: InterVarsity Press, 1996], 660).

responsible for Jesus' illegal execution.[32]

The Jews had also driven Paul and his companions out of Thessalonica and Berea, and then they had caused more trouble for him in Corinth (Acts 18:6, 12–16). The claim that the Jews "displease God and oppose all mankind" was rooted in the Jews' opposition to the evangelization of the Gentiles, and "to prohibit the preaching to the Gentiles was to stand in the way of the plan of God."[33] Moreover, it wasn't the apostle alone who shared this negative impression of his own countrymen; the Roman historian Tacitus (A.D. 56–117) would say of the Jews that "toward every other people they feel only hate and enmity," (*Histories* 5.5).[34]

The hatred and rebellion of the Jews accounted for the filling up the measure of their sins. The verb Paul uses in 2:16 "suggests the picture of a vessel or cup that is in a slow but constant process of being filled up, and once it is completely full, judgment will take place."[35] The idea of there being a fixed limit to a person's sins is reflected in Jewish literature (2 Esdras 4:34–37; 7:74; 2 Baruch 21:8; 48:2–5), as well as the OT. God did not allow Abraham's descendants to inherit Canaan until the sins of the Amorites had reached their full measure (Gen 15:16; cf. Dan 8:23). The author of 2 Maccabees wrote, "For in the case of the other nations the Lord waits patiently to punish them until they have reached the full measure of their sins" (6:14 NRSV). In a statement very similar to Paul's, Jesus ordered the religious leaders, "Fill up, then, the measure of your fathers" (Matt 23:32), a command that immediately preceded his accusation that the Jews had a

---

32. Acts 2:23, 36; 3:13–15; 4:10; 5:30; 7:52; 10:39; 13:28; cf. Mark 3:6; 14:1; 15:14–15; John 5:18; 7:1; 8:59; 11:45–53; 19:10–11.

33. Gene L. Green, *The Letters to the Thessalonians* (Grand Rapids: Eerdmans, 2002), 147.

34. See also the testimony of the Greek philosopher Philostratus (A.D. 160–245): "For the Jews have long been in revolt not only against the Romans, but against humanity; and a race that has made its own a life apart and irreconcilable, that cannot share with the rest of mankind in the pleasure of the table nor join in their libations or prayer or sacrifices, are separated from ourselves by a greater gulf than divides us from Susa or Bactra or the more distant Indies," (*Life of Apollonius* 5.33; cf. Diodorus Siculus 34.1.1–2).

35. CNTUOT 873.

long history of murdering men of God (Matt 23:33–36). Morris offers this helpful paraphrase of Paul's words: "They are seeing to it that nothing is left out in the catalogue of their sins!"[36]

The apostle's claim that "wrath has come upon them at last!" is difficult to adequately explain. For one thing, the phrase "at last" is more ambiguous than it might first appear (cf. "to the utmost," NASU). Does Paul mean that wrath has *finally* come, or that it has come *completely* with no alternative possible?[37] Considering how the phrase is used in Matt 10:22, Paul may mean that wrath has come upon the Jews "until the end" (cf. Rom 11:25–26).[38] In what way had wrath come upon the Jews when Paul wrote this letter? He could have been referring to the famine in A.D. 46 (cf. Acts 11:28), to the Jews being ordered to leave Rome in A.D. 49 (Acts 18:2; Suetonius, *Claudius* 25.4), to a brutal massacre of 20,000 Jews during Passover that same year (Josephus, *Antiquities* 20.105–6), or even to how God had hardened their hearts because the Jews had rejected Jesus.[39]

There is also a possibility Paul had a future event in mind, such as the destruction of Jerusalem and the Temple by the Romans in A.D. 70 (cf. Luke 21:20–24). Others believe that Paul is thinking both of the wrath to be poured out by God on unbelieving Jews in the here-and-now (e.g. destruction of Jerusalem), as well as in the hereafter (i.e. on Judgment Day).[40] The difficulty partially lies in the ambiguity of the verb "has come." Paul uses the Greek aorist tense, which usually denotes past action, but not always. Indeed, some argue that this is an example of the "prophetic past."[41]

---

36. Morris, *Thessalonians*, 85.

37. It's not out of the question that both meanings are intended here (Peter R. Ackroyd, "נצח—εἰς τέλος," *ExpTim* 80 [1968]: 126).

38. Witherington, *1 and 2 Thessalonians*, 88–89.

39. G. K. Beale, *1–2 Thessalonians* (Downers Grove, IL: InterVarsity Press, 200), 86–87.

40. "Uses of the verb *phthanō* in Matthew and Luke do not refer merely to an imminent future event but to something that has actually *begun to happen*, with more to come," (Ibid., 87).

41. "Paul is so certain of God's soon-coming judgment on his ancient people that he speaks of it—future though it still is—as an event that has already taken place," (Fee, *Thessalonians*, 102).

TALKING POINTS

P aul is very clear about his feelings on using deceit or trickery in evangelism. We may be fishers of men, but we are not to "bait" potential converts with gimmicks that appeal to base desires. After all, Jesus' bid to take up a cross daily (Luke 9:23) has to be the worst (and least manipulative) sales pitch ever. Wiersbe offers up this powerful reminder: "Salvation does not lie at the end of a clever argument or a subtle presentation. It is the result of God's Word and the power of the Holy Spirit," (1 Thess 1:5).[42] Neither does the salvation of the lost lie in a church having a prefect youth program, the most beautiful auditorium, or the most seeker-sensitive worship service. This is not to say these things are completely unimportant, but they are not the determining factor in whether someone accepts or rejects the gospel. Additionally, we must recall Paul's emphasis on his *conduct* and not just the *content* of his message. As I have often heard it put, some people will go to hell because they didn't know any Christians, while others will be there because they did.

P aul's declaration that he sought to please God is a statement pregnant with important implications. Church leaders need to think critically about the weight they lend to a "poll the audience" approach to decision-making. "The question men have too often asked is, 'What do I think?' instead of 'What does God say?' It is not our puny logic that matters; it is God's revelation."[43] I'm in no way suggesting that leaders should be insensitive or unconcerned with the thoughts and feelings of their followers. Equal caution, however, must be given to the other extreme, lest the tail wag the dog. At the end of the day, shepherds serve the Chief Shepherd and preachers serve the One who commissioned their message and mission. We labor and struggle and speak boldly and live out the implications of the gospel, knowing we must ultimately please God. Otherwise, we have failed spectacularly.

---

42. Wiersbe, *Be Ready*, 38.

43. Barclay, *Letters*, 191–92.

T here are several implications of Paul's statement in 1 Thess 2:14–16, but justification for anti-Semitism isn't one of them.[44] "Sadly, Christians have all too often been in the vanguard of hate and prejudice towards Jews."[45] Theological stalwarts like Martin Luther made severe anti-Semitic statements, but Chrysostom trumped everyone else when he preached eight sermons on this theme c. A.D. 386–88. These messages were caustic and poisonous, likening the Jews "to animals, and made wild accusations against them, ranging from gluttony, drunkenness and immorality to infanticide and even cannibalism."[46] Yes, our Lord was put to death in part by the Jews; it was the Jews who harassed the early church, and even Paul expresses his frustration with the Jews and their antagonism to the gospel. It is also true, however, that the church was exclusively Jewish until Acts 10. What is more, Paul later expressed his hope that the Jews would return to God (Rom 9–11). Whatever wrath exists for rebellious Jews at the end of time, God alone will administer it. All that is left to us is to love them, pray for them, and beckon them to obey the gospel of Jesus the Messiah.

---

44. "The man who wrote Rom. 9:1–5; 10:1 is hardly likely to have been guilty of anti-Semitism at any time," (Marshall, *1 and 2 Thessalonians*, 83).

45. Demarest, *1, 2 Thessalonians*, 63. "That many Christians persisted in anti-Judaism on theological grounds and still persist in it today can only be a cause for shame and repentance on the part of contemporary Christians," (Charles A. Wanamaker, *The Epistles to the Thessalonians* [Grand Rapids: Eerdmans, 1990], 119).

46. Stott, *Message of Thessalonians*, 58.

3

BROTHERS IN ARMS

In our society, we often idealize a strong person as independent—a maverick or lone-ranger type. We celebrate the rebel and glory in the individual triumphing over the masses. There may be nothing more crucial to the success of a group than the bond of love and unity between its individual members. A football team will never win a championship if players, intent on gaining individual accolades rather than contributing to the team's success, fracture its harmony. A military unit will lose the battle (and possibly their lives) unless they work together to achieve the objectives of their commander.

Barbara Streisand once sang, "People who need people are the luckiest people in the world." But I'd contend they are the *only* people in the world. Players on a sports team need each other. Soldiers in the trenches need to know they can rely on each other. Likewise, members of Christ's body need each other for support and confirmation that we're not alone in the Lord. Like an athlete or soldier, we rely on the person standing next to us to offer encouragement and love in times of turmoil.

Paul's need for his Christian family dominates this section of 1 Thessalonians. He loved these new Christians and longed to see them again, assuring them that he had attempted to return many times. I imagine the apostle spoke with a twinkle in his eye of that glorious day when he would be able to present them as a trophy to the Lord when Jesus returns.

Eventually, he was so desperate to hear from them that he was willing to allow Timothy, his right-hand man, to leave his side. The apostle's love for Timothy is also evident in this passage. Paul understood the importance of social interaction in sharing the gospel and thus warmly embraced his fellow Christians.

I grew up as a preacher's kid, so the church has always been a part of my life. There has never been a time when I was not a part of a local congregation. For that, I consider myself very blessed. Birthdays, holidays, and other special events were always celebrated with our church family. But those were the good times; never is the church more necessary to a Christian's survival than in bad times. Whether it's a terminal illness, unemployment, or a loved one's death, congregations are called to rally around those who hurt and manifest God's love in a powerful way.[1] When the church becomes a persecuted minority, its resilience is found in its love and unity.

Our need for one another is never more apparent than in the face of adversity. A very special bond is created between athletes when their team overcomes adversity and between troops when their unit is victorious over the enemy. The bond between Christian brethren is refined to the resilience of a thousand steel chains when they weather the hounds of hell. As a preacher, Paul believed in building his brethren up, rather than tearing them down. We are, after all, brothers in arms, serving a Commander who has never known defeat.

1 THESSALONIANS 2:17–20

When my father was six years old, he was abandoned to a children's home in Keller, Texas. His parents, both alcoholics, were going through a messy divorce. At an age when he could scarcely read or tie his shoes, my dad became an orphan. From time to time, he would speak of that dark

---

1.   In his book, *Where Is God When It Hurts?* author Philip Yancey's answer is, essentially, "In the church."

day in December 1965 when he and his siblings were ripped away from their parents. For a long time, he was haunted by the memory of his older and younger brothers, Nelson and Denny, screaming in the backseat as the car drove away. My dad, however, sat between them, saying nothing, internalizing it all. In some ways, the pain of that separation stayed with him for the rest of his life.

In 1 Thess 2:17, Paul's phrase "torn away" literally means "make an orphan"[2] (cf. John 14:18; Jas 1:27). In other words, he felt as if he had been ripped away from a loving family when forced to abruptly leave Thessalonica. The apostle assured his readers that their separation was only "for a short time" and "in person not in heart." Although he wasn't physically present with them during their affliction, he was there in spirit (cf. Gal 4:20), just as Christ is always present with his people (Matt 28:20). Paul had every intention of returning soon. In fact, he had already tried to do so on multiple occasions—"again and again" (2:18) actually means "several times but without an actual count."[3]

"But Satan hindered us," Paul says (cf. Rom 15:22). He uses a military verb here that signified destroying a road or bridge, thus impeding a pursuing enemy[4]—a particularly vivid and appropriate image in this context. Matthew Henry observed, "It is the devil's design to hinder the good fruit and effect of the preaching of the gospel. If he cannot hinder ministers from labouring in the word and doctrine, he will, if possible, hinder them of the success of their labours."[5] We don't know if the apostle is referring to religious harassment like he experienced from the

---

2. BDAG 119. "The natural sense of the verb shows that he is building on 2:7: now the little children have walked off and lost their parents," (Gary Shogren, 1 & 2 Thessalonians [Grand Rapids: Zondervan, 2012], 30).

3. Fee, Thessalonians, 106; cf. Leon Morris, "ΚΑΙ ΑΠΑΞ ΚΑΙ ΔΙΣ," NovT 1 (1956): 205–8.

4. NIDNTT 2:220.

5. Matthew Henry, Commentary on the Whole Bible, vol. 6 (New York: Revell, 1935), 779–80. Witherington likens Satan's hindering of the apostles' mission to Jesus' prevention in Acts 16:7. "Paul believes that supernatural forces are at work even in mundane events," (1 and 2 Thessalonians, 90).

Jews (2:14–16), a political injunction such as the ban on his returning to Thessalonica (cf. Acts 17:8–9), a physical ailment (cf. 2 Cor 12:7), or some other deterrent. I personally believe Paul is referring to the ban against his returning to the city. Timothy, however, was able to come and go since he was younger and likely enjoyed a lower profile, whereas Paul and Silas were much more recognizable. Regardless of how Paul was hindered, we know Satan was ultimately to blame.[6]

According to research done by The Barna Group in 2009, only 25% of self-identified Christians claim they believe in Satan. Compare that to 59% who strongly or somewhat agreed that Satan is a mere symbol of evil, rather than a living being.[7] Unfortunately, the reality of Satan is not dependent on polling data. Scripture assures us repeatedly that he is real.[8] I believe in Satan because Jesus did, and so did Paul—"For our struggle is not against flesh and blood, but against the rulers, against the authorities, against the powers of this dark world and against the spiritual forces of evil in the heavenly realms" (Eph 6:12 NIV). Martin Luther once quipped, "If you don't believe in the devil, it's because you've never tried to resist him."

To reinforce Paul's desire to return to Thessalonica, he makes a grandiose statement that borders on insincere exaggeration. "You are our hope, our joy, and the crown we will take pride in when our Lord Jesus Christ comes. Truly you are our glory and our joy" (1 Thess 2:19–20

---

6. "It is striking that Paul's references to Satan under one name or another appear in letters either written to Corinth (1 Cor 5:5; 7:5; 10:10; 2 Cor 2:11; 4:4; 6:15; 11:3, 14; 12:7) or from Corinth (Rom 16:20; 1 Thess 2:18; 2 Thess 2:9)," (Abraham J. Malherbe, *The Letters to the Thessalonians* [New York: Doubleday, 2000], 184).

7. The Barna Group, "Most American Christians Do Not Believe that Satan or the Holy Spirit Exist," http://www.barna.org/barna-update/article/12-faithspirituality/260-most-american-christians-do-not-believe-that-satan-or-the-holy-spirit-exis#.UqypgmRDvak (accessed December 14, 2013).

8. "A Western worldview shaped by Enlightenment views of science and nature is notoriously unsympathetic to the idea of spiritual beings. But such a naturalistic view of the universe (shaped by a mechanistic cause-and-effect understanding of reality) that disallows any place for spiritual beings also disallows any place for God," (Michael W. Holmes, *1 and 2 Thessalonians* [Grand Rapids: Zondervan, 1998], 105).

ncv). The glory and joy Paul speaks of here is the same experienced by parents as they hold their newborn in their arms; the same experienced by grandmothers as they make you swipe through endless photos of their "pride and joy." This is not an improper sinful pride that Paul speaks of, but an aggressive expression of joy and excitement over what God has done in the lives of the Thessalonians.[9] Compare this to the attitude of John in his letter to Gaius: "I have no greater joy than to hear that my children are walking in the truth" (3 John 4).

The "crown" mentioned in 2:19 is probably not the royal crown reserved for monarchs. Rather, it was a crown of reward made of laurel, pine needles, or oak leaves and awarded to athletic champions (cf. Isa 28:5; 62:3)—not that different from our Olympic gold medals. Traditionally, a Greek champion celebrated victory in the games by offering his crown to a deity (cf. Rev 4:10). This custom may be what Paul is invoking when he spoke of the return of Christ (cf. 1 Cor 9:24–27). "It is likely that Paul has in mind thoughts of joyfulness and victory" when he mentions this crown[10] (cf. Wisdom of Solomon 5:16; Sirach 47:6). Olympic champion Michael Phelps has more than twenty medals hanging on his mantle; he can point to these as proof of his domination in the sport of swimming during his career. In the same way, Paul pointed to the Thessalonians as unmitigated proof of his effective labor in the Kingdom (cf. Phil 4:1; 2 Tim 4:8; 1 Pet 5:4). Their success in faith made him eager to present them to Christ at his return.

1 THESSALONIANS 3:1–10

In the age of Skype and FaceTime, it's difficult to appreciate Paul's

---

9. Morris, *Thessalonians*, 90. Bruce harmonizes this boasting with Gal 6:14 in this way: "His glorying in his converts, as he saw the grace of God manifested in them, was but a phase of his paramount glorying in the cross. They were the fruit of the preaching of the cross," (*1 & 2 Thessalonians*, 58; cf. Fee, *Thessalonians*, 109–10).

10. Morris, *Thessalonians*, 90. The same Greek word is used of Jesus' crown of thorns (e.g. Matt 27:29; John 19:2, 5), which obviously epitomized the very opposite of joy and victory.

longing to see the Thessalonians in person or his resentment of Satan blocking his return. Eventually, it became too much. The phrase, "we could bear it no longer," carries with it the idea of something once watertight finally cracking and leaking.[11] Paul felt he had to do *something* about his concern for the Thessalonians, so he sent Timothy[12] to check on them and bring back a report.[13]

Each time Paul mentions Timothy to others, his praise of the young man is unequivocal. "I have no one else like Timothy, who genuinely cares about your welfare. All the others care only for themselves and not for what matters to Jesus Christ. But you know how Timothy has proved himself. Like a son with his father, he has served with me in preaching the Good News" (Phil 2:20–22 NLT; cf. 1 Cor 4:17; 16:10–11). In 1 Thess 3:2, Paul goes so far as to call Timothy "God's coworker in the gospel of Christ" (cf. 1 Cor 3:9; 2 Cor 6:1). Don't you mean *your* coworker, Paul? "No, Timothy is *God's* coworker." There is actually some debate as to whether Paul originally wrote "coworker" or "minister" (cf. KJV, NKJV).[14] Whatever he wrote, his point was that Timothy was invaluable in ministry. All God's ministers have the lofty privilege of serving alongside God to bring him glory and advance the cause of his gospel in the world (cf. 1 Cor 3:6).

If we wonder about the emotional toll Paul paid to go without Timothy for a time, we need only read those verses, not to mention 1–2 Timothy. Compounding Paul's sacrifice was the fact that he was alone once Timothy had left on his mission and in Athens no less. A city filled to the brim

---

11. TDNT 7:585–86; Bruce, *1 & 2 Thessalonians*, 60.

12. For more on Paul's use of messengers in his ministry, see Margaret M. Mitchell, "New Testament Envoys in the Context of Greco-Roman Diplomatic and Epistolary Conventions: The Example of Timothy and Titus," *JBL* 111 (1992): 641–62.

13. It can be confusing to harmonize Luke's account in Acts with Paul's account of events following his departure from Thessalonica. When all the data is assembled, however, it seems Paul came to Athens alone, having left Silas and Timothy in Berea. Once they reunited with him in Athens, Paul sent Timothy back to Thessalonica, while Silas went somewhere in Macedonia, maybe Philippi. They both were reunited once again in Corinth (ZIBBC 3:417).

14. Metzger, *Textual Commentary*, 563.

with so much vain philosophy and false religion must have drained Paul emotionally. His ministry does not seem to have borne the fruit there that it did elsewhere. In addition, his statement that he was "left behind" (3:1) carries overtones of "desertion or abandonment" (cf. Sirach 28:23).[15]

Paul hoped that his readers would not be "moved" by their trials, a verb that originally referred to a dog's wagging tail. It thus became a metaphor of flattery, deception,[16] and even of being upset or disturbed emotionally.[17] The apostle was concerned that the Thessalonians' social ostracism would become so weighty that their faith would fail them. Timothy's mission, then, was to establish and exhort the Thessalonians in their faith and to remind them of the things Paul had taught them. Basically, Timothy went back to Thessalonica to reenergize them with a pep talk, suggesting that it was possible for these Christians to have their faith shipwrecked and fall from grace (cf. Gal 5:4; 1 Tim 1:19–20), even though they were God's elect (1 Thess 1:4; 2 Thess 2:13).[18] Paul didn't want that to happen, so he sent his protégé "for fear that somehow the tempter had tempted you and our labor would be in vain" (1 Thess 3:5). "If Satan was blocking the apostles from entering Thessalonica, what dark deeds might he be doing behind those drawn curtains?"[19]

Note that Paul's fear was not that the Thessalonians might be persecuted. Particularly striking about the message Timothy brought to the Thessalonians was that, as members of the Lord's church, they were "destined for" affliction.[20] Time and again, the apostle and his

---

15. BDAG 521.

16. TDNT 7:54–56.

17. BDAG 910; H. Chadwick, "1 Thess. 3:3: σαίνεσθαι," *JTS* 1 (1950): 156–58.

18. "The danger of their succumbing to Satan was real, even though they had faith and even though he [Paul] prayed for them. It is not surprising, then, that a good deal of space in the letter is devoted to teaching and encouragement which will enable them to withstand the temptation to fall away from the faith," (I. Howard Marshall, "Election and Calling to Salvation in 1 and 2 Thessalonians" in *The Thessalonian Correspondence* [Leuven: Leuven Univ. Press, 1990], 262).

19. Shogren, *1 & 2 Thessalonians*, 138.

20. "The enduring of trials is a part of the appointed destiny of the people of God, not

companions had made this a core part of their preaching (Acts 14:22; Phil 1:29; 2 Thess 1:4–5; cf. 1 Pet 4:12–13). "Paul is not thinking of a period of persecution which will pass and the church return to normality; normality is persecution."[21] Paul was not afraid that Satan would devour the church through persecution, but rather that he would *use* persecution to *entice* the faithful away from God.

Are you OK with persecution and affliction being the Christian's destiny on earth? Are you at peace with suffering being a key requirement in the job description of living and longing for the Lord? Despite what a peddler of the Prosperity Gospel will tell you, suffering purifies us as God's people. Yes, Satan seeks to use it to destroy us. Through suffering, however, we identify with what Jesus endured on this earth (cf. Heb 12:2). In this way, the victory we will know at his return will be infinitely sweeter. Suffering confirms that we are truly members of Christ's body, the church (2 Tim 2:11–13; 3:12).

Timothy returned to Paul with overwhelmingly good news. No, Satan had not deceived and devoured them! Yes, their faith and love were increasing! No, they did not bear Paul ill will for his hasty departure! Instead, they remembered him "kindly"[22] and desperately wanted him to return. This brought tremendous comfort to Paul. You can almost hear his sigh of relief! "In all our distress and affliction we have been comforted about you through your faith" (1 Thess 3:7).[23] The apostle was overjoyed

---

because God seeks to punish us but because the world is alien to and resists the ways of God," (Woodson, *Perfecting Faith*, 59).

21. Ernest Best, *A Commentary on the First and Second Epistles to the Thessalonians* (Peabody, MA: Hendrickson, 1988), 135. "Tribulation is not to be wondered at by Christian people as though some strange and unusual happening befell them," (Morris, *Thessalonians*, 97).

22. Shogren argues that this "remembering" of Paul "refers to maintaining and practicing a teacher's model or pattern by the disciple ... The implication is: 'you maintain a good memory of us always and use that mental picture as a guide for your own actions,' (*1 & 2 Thessalonians*, 140).

23. "Now that Timothy has come and reported good news about them, Paul intensifies his description of his distress, thereby heightening the comfort that Timothy's report brought to him," (Malherbe, *Thessalonians*, 202).

and knew where to direct his thanksgiving—not just to the Thessalonians, but also (and ultimately) to God.[24] He spoke of trying to repay God in prayer for what the Lord had done among the Thessalonians. Of course, the apostle knew that adequately repaying the Giver of every good and perfect gift is impossible.[25] So he prayed "earnestly"[26] and "night and day" to be allowed to return to Thessalonica, which was expressive of just how devoted Paul was to achieving this goal (cf. Pss 22:2; 42:8; 63:6; 77:2, 6; 119:55, 148).

In 3:10, he mentions his desire to supply what was lacking in the Thessalonians' faith. Although there was much to commend in his readers, there were also some things that needed to be rectified, and it is to these things that Paul turns in the next chapter. The verb translated "make up" means "to cause to be in a condition to function well,"[27] and is used elsewhere of repairing nets (Matt 4:21), as well as men (Gal 6:1). The absence of certain qualities didn't mean the Thessalonians were poor Christians, but Paul knew that we never "arrive" as true Christians this side of eternity. The process of becoming more like Jesus is one that lasts until death or the Lord calls our name.

1 THESSALONIANS 3:11–13

Paul wraps up this first section of the letter with a prayer (cf. Eph 3:20–21; 2 Thess 2:16–17), one that summarizes much of what he has said thus far. His prayer is honest and specific, beseeching God to frustrate Satan's resistance and direct Paul's return to the Thessalonians (cf. Num

---

24. Paul's question in 3:9, "what thanksgiving can we return to God for you," is better translated "How can we thank God enough for you?" (NIV). The question is rhetorical—"The meaning is that no thanksgiving we are able to render can ever be adequate," (Whiteley, *Thessalonians*, 54).

25. Fee, *Thessalonians*, 126.

26. This word means "quite beyond all measure" and is the "highest form of comparison imaginable," (BDAG 1033). It appears in the NT only one other time (Eph 3:20).

27. BDAG 526.

6:24–26; Ps 20:1–5). It is not insignificant that the apostle responded to Satan's work with prayer.

> Whatever power Satan possesses is real, but Paul believes that it will prove no match for the power of God. It is God alone who will finally triumph. ... Paul and his colleagues will not return to Thessalonica simply by planning their itineraries more carefully. Nor will the Thessalonians experience enhanced community life or moral practices because they will themselves to do so. These things come about not as achievements but as gifts of God.[28]

Paul also wanted the Thessalonians' love "for one another and for all" to increase and abound, two synonymous verbs that Paul uses for emphasis. It's one thing to love our Christian family; it is quite another to love those inflicting persecution and affliction on us. "How the Christian community in Thessalonica related to outsiders is to Paul no less important than how they related to each other," (cf. Phil 2:15).[29] As Wiersbe puts it, "Times of suffering can be times of selfishness. Persecuted people often become very self-centered and demanding."[30] Paul, however, wished that they would grow in their love for their enemies, a central tenet of Jesus' teaching (Matt 5:43–46; 24:10, 12). This second request was evidently answered quickly (2 Thess 1:3), but it would be several years before Paul actually returned to Thessalonica (Acts 20:1–2).

It is important to note that this prayer is addressed to both "our God and Father" and "our Lord Jesus."[31] Paul did not do this in an overt way (as if he had a Trinitarian axe to grind), but very casually. "Here is a strict

---

28. Gaventa, *Thessalonians*, 47.

29. Holmes, *1 and 2 Thessalonians*, 115.

30. Wiersbe, *Be Ready*, 67.

31. In 3:11, Paul "links the two [i.e. the Father and the Son] by making them the joint subject of a verb that is in the singular," (Morris, *Thessalonians*, 107). The awkward grammar might be reflected in English in this way: "We hope the Father and the Son directs us to you ..."

monotheist praying with ease to both the Father and the Son, focusing first on the one and then the other, and without a sense that his monotheism is being stretched or is in some kind of danger."[32] A Gentile like me might not think much of it, but this would have been a classic stumbling block for any monotheistic Jew who prayed the Shema each day—"Hear, O Israel: The LORD our God, the LORD is one" (Deut 6:4). At other times, Paul would address his prayer to the Father alone (1:2–3; 5:23) or to the Son alone (2 Thess 3:5, 16). To teach that it is a sin to pray to one member of the Trinity, but not the other, is to contradict the apostle's example.[33]

In the beginning of 1 Thess 4, Paul embarks on a discussion addressing what was lacking in the Thessalonians' faith. They needed to work at putting into practice those commands that Paul gave them, so he uses a phrase in this prayer, reminding us that becoming more like Jesus is in fact God's work. It is God who teaches us to love even our tormenters. Learning to love apart from God is "a bit like trying to find water in the desert without a well."[34] Ultimately, it is God who establishes our "hearts blameless in holiness before our God and Father" (3:13).[35]

Besides his own salvation, Paul's ultimate desire was to see the Thessalonians prepared for that great day when Christ returns "with all his holy ones" (NIV), meaning angels (cf. Matt 25:31).[36] Paul's quote here

---

32. Fee, *Thessalonians*, 130–31.

33. "Integral to the apostle's theology is that Paul prays to the Lord Jesus just as he prays to the Father. He does not defend or justify the practice. We can only assume that the new disciples had heard him praying to God the Father and to the Lord Jesus from the very first. There is syntactical tension here that reveals something of his theology; technically there is disagreement between the plural subjects 'our God and Father *and* our Lord Jesus' and the singular verbs of which they are the subject. In English we would have to imagine a sentence such as 'God and Jesus directs us' in order to hear the same grammatical discord. It is common in the Pauline literature to see Jesus assume many of the roles of God," (Shogren, *1 & 2 Thessalonians*, 143).

34. Demarest, *1, 2 Thessalonians*, 70.

35. "The focus here is not on what God does to his people at the end of history but on God's work in the lives of his people *until* they share Christ's glory at his final coming," (Beale, *1–2 Thessalonians*, 111).

36. "The problem with arguing that saints are meant by 'holy ones' here … is that the

is actually lifted from Zech 14:5, "Then the LORD my God will come, and all the holy ones with him."[37] In the OT, "holy ones" referred to angels,[38] and since Jesus promised he would return with his angels (Matt 13:41; Mark 8:38; 13:26–27; cf. 2 Thess 1:7; Jude 14), it seems appropriate to interpret "saints" or "holy ones" as angels.

That said, I believe there is an intentional play on words here between "holiness" and "holy ones." To eagerly expect Jesus' imminent return—to long for the Lord—inspires us to live for him and walk in holiness, for our sanctification will be consummated only on that great and final day (Phil 1:6). Paul wanted the Thessalonians to see the connection between living in holiness and being prepared for the appearance of the Holy One and his holy ones in the sky. How crucial such a vision was to their survival in a pagan, immoral culture! If the church today were to recapture this eager longing for Christ's return in its hymns, prayers, admonition, encouragement, and teaching, imagine the difference it would make in our living for the Lord in such a hostile society!

---

saints will reunite with Jesus when he comes, not before," (Witherington, *1 and 2 Thessalonians*, 104). For the view that interprets "holy ones" as Christians, see CNTUOT 875; Comfort, "1 & 2 Thessalonians," 355–56. Morris believes both meanings are intended: "In this particular case there seems to be no reason for holding that Paul's thought is limited to one class of the other," (*Thessalonians*, 111).

37. Again, that Paul substituted "our Lord Jesus" for "the LORD my God" is not insignificant.

38. e.g. Deut 33:3; Job 5:1; 15:15; Ps 89:4–7; Dan 4:13; 8:13.

TALKING POINTS

Paul saw opposition as the work of Satan, not just people. We, too, need to look at things through spiritual eyes (Eph 6:12). I'm not advocating that we use this as an excuse (cf. Flip Wilson's mantra, "The devil made me do it"), but rather that we should take responsibility for our actions. Personal accountability, along with confessing that there is very dark and powerful evil in the world, are not mutually exclusive endeavors. "We pay a high price ... for our unwillingness to speak about evil, for by so doing we implicitly deny that it exists."[39] This is particularly important for church leaders and ministers. Whenever conflict or disruptions arise, we must remember that lurking behind every sinful action is the evil one—Satan is the true enemy! Moreover, we should adopt Paul's strategy in recognizing prayer as arguably the most potent weapon in our arsenal. Finally, we should trust in God that the difficulties we face, and however long we face them, are for our good. As we learn in Job's story (e.g. 1:12; 2:6), Satan can do no more harm than God allows.[40]

In spite of the opposition Satan mounts against us, we mysteriously can still trust that God's providence remains at work for our good and his glory. "God remains sovereign even over present dark frustrations."[41] Paul longed to be reunited with the Thessalonians like parents separated from their children. He also knew that the temporary separation was Satan's work and prayed for God to remove the obstacles (1 Thess 3:11). But if it had not been for this temporary separation, two millennia of Christians would not have benefited from the letters we now know as 1–2 Thessalonians.[42] The next time you desire something with a godly longing, but believe Satan is

---

39. Gaventa, *Thessalonians*, 43.

40. Shogren, *1 & 2 Thessalonians*, 134.

41. Tom Wright, *Paul for Everyone: Galatians and Thessalonians* (Louisville: Westminster John Knox, 2004), 106. "In this spiritual warfare, Satan is hardly an omnipotent adversary. But he is a real adversary," (Green, *Thessalonians*, 152).

42. Comfort, "1 & 2 Thessalonians," 353.

throwing up obstacles to frustrate you, know that God may be saying "not yet" in order to implement his perfect plan. Who is to say two millennia's worth of Christians will not benefit from your patience?

D o you consider your fellow Christians to be your brothers in arms? An athlete intent on victory must care about the well being of his teammates. A soldier who wants to win—not simply survive—the battle must care about the readiness of his comrades. In the same way, Christians must care about one another's spiritual welfare enough to pray for them "earnestly" both "night and day." Too often, we engage in prayer from a purely selfish position. We might pray for someone when they are facing surgery or a terminal illness, but how often do we engage in persistent, enthusiastic prayer for others?[43] And what of joy? "Are we like Paul? Do we get our greatest joy from seeing brethren remain faithful and grow spiritually? When are we the most encouraged? Is it when the church makes forward strides or when our favorite sporting team wins?"[44] What a convicting thought! May God help us find inexpressible, obnoxious joy in his people, and may he help us to realize how difficult it is to maintain petty differences when we give thanks and pray for others so fervently.

---

43. "We will never know from how much sin we have been saved and how much temptation we have conquered all because someone prayed for us. It is told that once a servant-girl became a member of a Church. She was asked what Christian work she did. She said that she had not have the opportunity to do much because her duties were so constant but, she said, 'When I go to bed I take the morning newspaper to my bed with me; and I read the notices of the births and I pray for all the little babies; and I read the notices of marriage and I pray that those who have been married may be happy; and I read the announcements of death and I pray that the sorrowing may be comforted.' No man can ever tell what tides of grace flowed from her attic bedroom," (Barclay, *Letters*, 196).

44. Edwards, *1 & 2 Thessalonians*, 96.

4

WALK THIS WAY

In early December 2013, news spread around the world of Nelson Mandela's death. President Mandela was a prominent leader on the world stage, famous for leading the very country that had imprisoned him for so many years. During the memorial service for President Mandela, however, a national embarrassment occurred in front of nearly a hundred international heads of state, one seemingly too ridiculous to be true.

The sign language interpreter on stage, Thamsanqa Jantjie, proved to be a fake. During the service, he made meaningless hand gestures that did not resemble sign language at all. How Jantjie had been able to get the gig was anyone's guess. A South African association for the deaf was outraged and accused Jantjie of making a "mockery of South African sign language."[1] Two days later, Jantjie apologized. The reason for the outrage was simple: Thamsanqa Jantjie had failed miserably to act in a way consistent with who he claimed to be, and his signs did not match what was being expressed by speakers at President Mandela's memorial. There was a significant gap between claim and reality.

Like Jantjie, some self-pronounced Christians live as frauds or hypocrites. We can claim to be followers of Christ, but show an inability or unwillingness to live in a way that validates our claim. Put another way,

---

1. John Eligon, "Interpreter at Memorial Service Said to Have Been an Impostor," *New York Times*, December 11, 2013.

our "signs" don't match what what the Word of God has expressed.

With the beginning of 1 Thess 4, Paul turns his attention to instructing the Thessalonians in various matters.[2] Whenever he broached the subject of Christian behavior in his letters, the apostle made it clear that such behavior is to be based on our calling. "As a prisoner for the Lord, then, I urge you to live a life worthy of the calling you have received" (Eph 4:1 NIV). The commands given in 1 Thess 4:1–12 follow the same reasoning. The apostle wanted the Thessalonians to walk their talk, to be authentic and consistent expressions of what God was saying. Specifically in this passage, Paul's instructions grew out of his desire to complete what was lacking in his readers' faith (3:10). Before transitioning to an extended discussion related to the Second Coming, Paul addressed the very practical matters of sex, love, and work.

1 THESSALONIANS 4:1–2

Paul introduces this new section in a very diplomatic way. He wants to address a few critical issues, but he doesn't want to discourage his readers. The Thessalonians are doing well, but he wants them to lead a pleasing life before God "more and more."[3] J. W. Shepherd put it this way: "There is no finality to progressive holiness while the believer remains on earth. Life is marked either by growth or decay."[4]

Inspired writers often employed walking language to express a lifestyle (e.g. Gen 5:24; 6:9; Deut 5:33). In Paul's letters alone, the expression occurs more than thirty times. If his words had only been about how we walk/live, it would have been sufficient, but he also throws in the phrase "please God" (cf. Rom 8:8). I love this addition! It is a reminder that Christians are not

---

2. "Throughout this letter his concern for spiritual advance in the Thessalonian church has surfaced a number of times, but now he gives it more concentrated attention," (Morris, *Thessalonians*, 113).

3. "To sit back satisfied with what one has done is to sound the death knell of effective Christian service," (Ibid., 129).

4. Lipscomb, *Commentary*, 45.

called to adhere to an arbitrary moral code, nor do we live or behave so as to bring ourselves personal satisfaction or to enjoy the esteem of others. If our motivation to live a Christian lifestyle were this selfish, we would inevitably fail. Perfection in life is impossible to achieve as it is. If our character is dependent on ever-changing whims, or on how many people are watching us, it will only be a matter of time before we fail a moral code.[5]

Christians must live to please the Lord, just as Jesus lived to please the Father (John 8:29). We have been wired to serve a higher purpose than ourselves, for "to please God is the highest ambition of the true Christian; the consciousness of pleasing him is the highest Christian joy."[6] Pleasing God is the doorway to the abundant life Jesus promised (John 10:10);[7] living any other way leads to death and destruction. Most importantly, living so as to please the Lord reminds us that life is about bringing God glory. "'Pleasing God' does not mean anything so mundane as 'being pleasant' toward him but rather points to serving him in a way that makes his interests a person's primary ambition."[8] When our supreme desire is to please the Lord, everything else will matter little or not at all to us.

Paul reminds the Thessalonians that they knew the right way to live. The apostle and his companions had not only modeled the Christian life for them, but the Thessalonians had been taught "instructions ... through the Lord Jesus" (4:2). Referring to these as "instructions" doesn't do justice to the Greek word Paul uses, a military term "with a ring of authority" to it[9] (cf. Acts 5:28; 16:24). That's why "commands" (HCSB) or "commandments" (NASU) provides a better, more nuanced translation.

---

5. "An additional feature worth noticing in these verses is that they offer no promise of a reward in exchange for an acceptable moral life. No carrot swings from the end of this text. Paul assumes that believers want to please God, not that they do so in order to get the prize at the bottom of the box," (Gaventa, *Thessalonians*, 50).

6. Lipscomb, *Commentary*, 45.

7. Morris, *Thessalonians*, 116.

8. Green, *Thessalonians*, 185.

9. "It is this which makes it suitable for this context where Paul is stressing the authoritative nature of the injunctions in question," (Morris, *Thessalonians*, 116).

1 THESSALONIANS 4:3-8

When Paul sent his correspondence to Thessalonica, he was staying in Corinth. The sexual immorality[10] of that city is well documented (e.g. 1 Cor 5; 6:12–20), but this type of depravity wasn't limited to first-century Corinth. Sexual immorality was epidemic throughout Greco-Roman culture due to their lenient laws and obsession with decadence. Even after their conversion, it remained a problem for Gentile Christians. "Among the Jews marriage was theoretically held in the highest esteem. It was said that a Jew must die rather than commit murder, idolatry or adultery."[11] Divorce was a problem among the Jews, as was lust (Matt 5:31–32; 19:1–9), but these seem to have been the general extent of their sexual immorality.

The Gentiles, however, were an entirely different story (cf. Acts 15:20, 29). Single Greek men often engaged in hetero- and homosexual acts with multiple partners since their religion did not provide a disincentive for doing so.[12] Roman marriage contracts, for example, gave husbands license for extramarital affairs as long so they were not with other men's wives.[13] In the fourth century B.C., the Athenian orator Demosthenes quipped, "Mistresses we keep for the sake of pleasure, concubines for the daily care of our persons, but wives to bear us legitimate children and to be faithful guardians of our households," (*Against Neaera* 122).[14] So

---

10. "Paul's condemnation of extramarital sex was sweeping and unqualified. When he used the term *porneia* [as in 1 Thess 4:3], Paul's meaning was unequivocal—it embraced any and all sexual relationships outside of marriage," (James A. Brundage, *Law, Sex, and Christian Society in Medieval Europe* [Chicago: Univ. of Chicago Press, 1987], 61; cf. J. Jensen, "Does Porneia Mean Fornication? A Critique of Bruce Malina," *NovT* 20 [1978]: 161–84).

11. Barclay, *Letters*, 198.

12. Craig S. Keener, *The IVP Bible Background Commentary: New Testament* (Downers Grove, IL: InterVarsity Press, 1993), 590.

13. Comfort, "1 & 2 Thessalonians," 359. He goes on to acknowledge that Augustus prohibited all adultery in A.D. 18, but that "the law's effectiveness in restraining it was questionable."

14. "If there is anyone who thinks that youth should be forbidden affairs even with courtesans, … his view is contrary not only to the license of this age but also to the customs and concessions of our ancestors. For when was this not a common practice? When was it blamed?

great was the stigma of sexual immorality among the Gentiles that Jewish rabbis believed a Gentile woman's virginity couldn't be assumed if she were more than three years and one day old.[15] The rabbis had a penchant for over-exaggeration, but their point retains its emphasis.

In the strongest language possible,[16] Paul dictated that sexual purity is "the will of God" and our "sanctification," and that we are to "abstain"[17] from any sexual activity that does not honor God. Christians are expected to control their bodies, rather than giving in to "the passion of lust like the Gentiles who do not know God" (cf. Ps 79:6; Jer 10:25; Rom 1:24; 1 Cor 1:21; Gal 4:8; Col 3:5; 2 Thess 1:8). The phrase "passion of lust" invokes a situation "in which indulgence of physical desires has taken control of the person and he or she has abandoned all restraints against gratifying such desires."[18] Whiteley describes this as "'pathological lust', lust so extreme that a man is not master of it, but is swept down by a Niagara of desire."[19] Such unrestrained passion is incompatible in the Christian's life since we know God, and have thus been called to holiness (4:7) and given God's Spirit (4:8).[20] If a Christian does not allow God to restrain his lust,

---

When was it forbidden?" (Cicero, *In Defense of Marcus Caelius Rufus* 48).

15. Keener, *Bible Background*, 591.

16. "The language of this passage could not be weightier or more emphatic. Though Paul employs euphemisms in describing sexual sin, he speaks with great plainness about what God expects and the consequences of disobedience," (Green, *Thessalonians*, 201).

17. Stott argues that "abstain" or "avoid" (NIV) are not strong enough translations in this particular instance. "The apostle is declaring that God's will entails 'a clean cut' with impurity, a total abstinence," (*Message of Thessalonians*, 82). "Paul does not call the church to partial moderation of their sexual impulses but to abstain completely from all forms of *sexual immorality*," (Green, *Thessalonians*, 190–91).

18. Woodson, *Perfecting Faith*, 67. "Passion signifies an overpowering feeling, one to which one so yields himself that he is borne along by evil as if he were its passive instrument; he has lost the dignity of self-control and is the slave of his own appetites," (Lipscomb, *Commentary*, 46).

19. Whiteley, *Thessalonians*, 61.

20. "The Christian ethic has its foundation in God, who not only makes his will known but whose presence is powerful in their lives through the Holy Spirit. Therefore, disobedience to the divine imperative was a negation of the indicative of their relationship with God," (Green,

what a terrible testimony he bears to the world!

It is possible that an extramarital affair was going on in the Thessalonian church.[21] Paul spells out the seriousness of such a sin by using familial terms. Adultery is anything but a victimless crime.[22] It is a violation of the Golden Rule; when a man sleeps with another's wife, he is guilty of trespassing.[23] Adultery within the church is also tantamount to incest; adultery within the church fails to appreciate the familial relationship Christians enjoy as true brothers and sisters in the family of God—something we should never take lightly.[24] Not even sexual activity with a non-Christian partner before marriage is exempt from the call to sexual holiness. Such activity robs both parties of their virginity, which rightly belongs to future spouses. Those future spouses have "been defrauded. And, of course, if a child is born as the result of this sin, the little one bears the stigma of illegitimacy."[25]

Paul solemnly warned that the sexually immoral would experience God's wrath (cf. Eph 5:5–6; Col 3:5–6). The vengeance he speaks of here is not petty or capricious—violators of sexual purity have not rejected Paul, but God himself (cf. Luke 10:16). God always works to bring relief to the oppressed, for he is a God of justice (cf. Ps 94). Note, however, that Paul speaks of "the Lord" (likely meaning Christ) as an avenger, and that this vengeance may not be reserved for the end of time. The apostle is

---

Thessalonians, 201).

21. "The serious and even threatening tone of vv. 6–8 suggests very strongly that Paul was dealing with a problem that had actually emerged in the community at Thessalonica," (Wanamaker, *Thessalonians*, 158).

22. "What many would view in our day as a strictly 'personal' issue is understood by the apostle as a community issue that has eternal consequences," (Green, *Thessalonians*, 197).

23. The force of the Greek term translated "transgress" "is of crossing ... a forbidden boundary, and hence trespassing (sexually) on territory which is not one's own," (Bruce, *1 & 2 Thessalonians*, 84).

24. "When Christians engage in sexual adventurism with another believer, they have ceased to behave as they should act toward a sibling," (Shogren, *1 & 2 Thessalonians*, 166).

25. Morris, *Thessalonians*, 124.

purposefully using legal terminology; just as civil government punishes the wicked and avenges their crime (Rom 13:4), so too does God avenge the injustice[26] of sexual immorality (2 Thess 1:8). We have all heard about those who rejected God's will concerning their sexuality and, as a result, destroyed happy marriages and families, to say nothing of contracting diseases that ruined their bodies and haunted them the rest of their lives. The here-and-now consequences of sin, however, pale in comparison to the wrath stored up for the sexually immoral on the final day (Rev 21:8).

Several years ago in a particular congregation, a man and a woman (both married, although not to one another) had an affair. When it came to light, they refused to repent. Instead, they divorced their respective spouses and married one another. They continued for a time in that congregation, maintaining a lack of godly sorrow for their actions, before moving away for unrelated reasons. Needless to say, they left behind a great deal of pain in the wake of their selfishness. Families were destroyed, children traumatized, and the church was divided. Many years later, these painful scars remained. It was to avoid such unnecessary pain that Paul spoke so vehemently on this issue.

A very perplexing part of this passage is found in 1 Thess 4:4, which Shogren calls "the most complex verse in the Thessalonian correspondence."[27] The difficulty resides in the fact that both the verb ("control" ESV; "possess" NASU; "take" RSV) and the noun ("body" ESV; "vessel" NASU; "wife" RSV) have debatable meanings. The noun *skeuos* simply means a "container" or "jar," while the verb *ktaomai* means to acquire or possess.[28] As you will see, none of the following interpretive

26. "'Avenger' ... does not carry the sense of 'getting even,' only the administration of true justice," (Edwards, *1 & 2 Thessalonians*, 125).

27. Shogren, *1 & 2 Thessalonians*, 161.

28. BDAG 572.

options emerge as a clear consensus since each has its own problems.[29]

- *Skeuos* as a reference to one's body. There are a few examples of *skeuos* holding this meaning; passages such as Acts 9:15 and 2 Cor 4:7 are often suggested as evidence of this definition, but it's not clear that the human body is being discussed here. In addition, "control" is not the normal translation of the Greek verb.

- The phrase collectively refers to a man taking a wife (cf. 1 Pet 3:7) according to God's design. This is certainly how early Christian writers interpreted the verse. But 1 Pet 3:7 infers that both the man and the woman are vessels, instead of the wife being the husband's vessel. If Paul meant "wife" when he used the noun *skeuos*, why didn't he instead use the Greek *gynē* (cf. "gynecology") as he did in 1 Cor 7:2? Also, to speak of a wife as one's "vessel" is, in Lightfoot's words, a "low sensual view of the marriage relation" and a "depreciatory estimate of the woman's position."[30]

- *Skeuos* as a euphemism for the male genitals (cf. 1 Sam 21:5 LXX). Witherington notes that Paul uses other words elsewhere for genitalia (e.g. 1 Cor 12:23–24), and those words are not used 1 Thess 4:4.[31] Also, Fee notes that the verb "acquire" is incompatible and nonsensical with this interpretation.[32]

This is yet another situation where we could very easily miss the forest for the trees. The broader meaning of the passage is not eclipsed by lexical difficulty. Paul is saying that every Christian (male and female)

---

29. Shogren offers the best discussion of the options, though he concludes that none "is the obvious victor," (*1 & 2 Thessalonians*, 162–64; cf. Malherbe, *Thessalonians*, 226–28).

30. Lightfoot, *Notes*, 55.

31. Witherington, *1 and 2 Thessalonians*, 113–14.

32. He does, however, argue that "to gain mastery over" is a legitimate translation of the Greek verb (Fee, *Thessalonians*, 149).

must control themselves and honor God in their sexuality, a message that is as relevant today as it was in the first century.

1 THESSALONIANS 4:9–12

Paul had other concerns for the newly converted Thessalonians, specifically whether they would continue to grow in their love for one another[33] and live quietly. "Brotherly love" is what Paul sought to foster—as you might guess, the Greek term *philadelphia* is used. In the ancient world, *philadelphia* was mostly limited to the love between family members[34] (cf. 4 Maccabees 13:21, 23, 26; 14:1; 15:10; Philo, *On the Embassy to Gaius* 87, 92). While modern Christians may think nothing of it, early Christians would have been surprised by how often *philadelphia* was used to characterize their relationships with one another.[35] Some would have no doubt considered it an undue imposition to love fellow Christians to this degree, especially when their culture made no such demands. The church of Jesus Christ has always been a group of people from varied racial, political, and socio-economic backgrounds, and brotherly love—a love taught to us by God himself—has always been the glue binding us inextricably together through the worst of trials. Two manifestations of this form of love were hospitality and generosity towards others, two things at which the Thessalonians particularly excelled (2 Cor 8:1–5). Perhaps this should cause some of us to pause and reevaluate the love we have for our own brethren, as well as the lengths to which we go to express that love, lest it always remain abstract.

Love is not something that comes naturally to a person, but is a part of the Spirit's fruit in our lives (Gal 5:22; cf. 1 Cor 2:13). It is our Father

---

33. "The thought is of mutual love, as contrasted with the usual word for love, *agapē*, which can signify unrequited love," (Marshall, *1 and 2 Thessalonians*, 114).

34. Fee, *Thessalonians*, 159; Shogren, *1 & 2 Thessalonians*, 167. For a terrific window into the use of this word, see Hans Dieter Betz, "De Fraterno Amore (Moralia 478A–492D)" in *Plutarch's Ethical Writings and Early Christian Literature* (Leiden: Brill, 1978), 231–63.

35. cf. Rom 8:29; 12:9–10; Gal 6:10; Heb 13:1; 1 Pet 1:22; 2:17; 3:8; 2 Pet 1:7.

who teaches us to love one another (Ps 16:7; Isa 54:13; Jer 31:33–34; John 6:45). He helps our love grow "more and more" (1 Thess 4:10) by putting us in situations where we must *learn* to love. Ask a football coach how to become a better blocker or tackler, and he'll tell you to practice blocking and tackling—practice makes perfect. Take a moment to reflect on the love we have for one another, as well as the lengths to which we will go to express that love. Do we practice it regularly, or only when it is mandatory? Do we keep it in our hearts, strengthening it through word and action? Or do we allow it to remain an abstract concept because it is too time-consuming or difficult to practice?

In the life of the church, there is a constant stream of circumstances where genuine brotherly love is necessary. Unfortunately, these usually involve conflict. We shouldn't go looking for conflict, but neither should we avoid it. Mature Christians will recognize conflict as an opportunity to flex the spiritual muscles of love. Addressing and resolving conflict in a godly way assures that brotherly love in a church will grow "more and more."[36] Christians should recognize these opportunities when they come and earnestly discern how brotherly love needs to be shown.

In addition to love, the apostle calls his readers to live quietly, to mind their own business, and to work with their hands. This is a brief allusion to the problem of idleness in Thessalonica, which receives much fuller attention in 2 Thess 3:6–15. Paul, however, argues here that being responsible and living quietly is an outgrowth of *philadelphia*—"Love for one another also means not to impose on others' kindness."[37]

Paul intentionally uses an oxymoron when he says we should "Be ambitious to be quiet," or "Seek strenuously to be still,"[38] (cf. 1 Tim 2:2). The apostle used very similar language elsewhere when explaining that his

---

36. Wiersbe, *Be Ready*, 78–79.

37. Gordon D. Fee and Douglas Stuart, *How to Read the Bible Book by Book* (Grand Rapids: Zondervan, 2002), 372.

38. Morris, *Thessalonians*, 131. "Paul here combines words of contradictory meaning in order to give point and force to the exhortation," (Lipscomb, *Commentary*, 51).

ambition was to both spread the gospel (Rom 15:20) and please the Lord (2 Cor 5:9). He is warning against a lifestyle that seeks joy or fulfillment in the here-and-now. The Greek term translated "to live quietly" was one that, for a long time, "described withdrawal from active participation in political and social affairs."[39] I'm not going to say that Paul's words here prohibit Christians from being political or social activists.[40] There is, after all, that little reference about being salt and light (Matt 5:13–16). Nonetheless, it would do every Christian good to think through the implications of the command to live quietly, to not draw attention to oneself, and to work diligently so as to attract outsiders (4:12), thereby glorifying and pleasing the Lord in all things. Recall that Paul and his associates had been accused of upsetting the world (Acts 17:6); in light of this, the Thessalonian Christians had no margin for error. The same Lord who called his followers to be salt and light also taught them to turn the other cheek when their dignity and civil liberties were violated (Matt 5:38–41).

The command to mind their own business and work diligently in order to provide for themselves is surely addressed to the unruly. Paul later addresses these folks in a more direct manner, but note again that this command is an outgrowth of brotherly love. Some Christians seemingly have a compulsive need to know what is going on with everyone else, but we must remember that "believers who are about the Father's business

---

39. Malherbe, *Thessalonians*, 241. "The expressions 'to live quietly' and 'to tend to one's own affairs' go together and have unmistakable political connotations … When Paul's readers had converted to Christianity, as has previously been observed, a public outcry arose and resulted in oppressive measures against them (cf. 1:6; 2:14; 3:3f.). Whether willingly or unwillingly, they had come into public view and had suffered for their faith. Thus Paul's exhortation to them 'to aspire to live quietly and to mind your own affairs' was an eminently practical piece of advice. He hoped that by maintaining a low profile they would avoid further trouble for themselves," (Wanamaker, *Thessalonians*, 162–63).

40. "Commentators have been hesitant to interpret this precept in political terms, preferring to view Paul's advice in terms of church affairs. The language, however, is unmistakably political," (Ronald F. Hock, *The Social Context of Paul's Ministry* [Philadelphia: Fortress, 1980], 46). Green has no such scruples: "We can safely assume that the apostle is calling believers to stay out of public/political affairs," (*Thessalonians*, 210).

(Luke 2:49) do not have the time—or desire—to meddle in the affairs of others."[41]

There is surely something in this passage that speaks to America's love affair with consumerism. So often, we purchase things we don't need with money we don't have. When we are neither diligent workers, nor responsible with our finances, it's inevitable that we will have to impose on others and become dependent on their generosity. What kind of example does this set for the pagan world around us?

I know a gentleman who was notorious in the congregation for approaching brethren (often new members) and asking for a few hundred dollars. To one brother, he was in debt to the tune of tens of thousands of dollars. One can imagine the strain it placed on the whole congregation, not to mention this man's relationships with his brothers and sisters. Apparently, the implications of brotherly love reach much farther than we initially think.[42]

41. Wiersbe, *Be Ready*, 80.

42. "It is an expression of love to support others who are in need; but it is also an expression of love to support ourselves, so as not to need to be supported by others," (Stott, *Message of Thessalonians*, 90).

TALKING POINTS

It is alarming to me that such significant strides have been made to legitimize homosexuality in my lifetime. Those Christians advocating that the church should no longer condemn the practice of homosexuality should be ashamed of themselves. But so also should Christians who undermine God's call to "abstain from sexual immorality," a call that encompasses more than just homosexuality. Many churches have become overly tolerant or kept silent concerning this call. Study after study shows that half of all Christian men, and about 20% of women, confessed to viewing Internet pornography in the last year. Divorce rates in the Bible Belt are higher than anywhere else in the United States. Some of the most conservative churches I know have been plagued for decades with a high rate of teen pregnancies. As far as adultery, church discipline is often non-existent. We cannot idly accept the status quo, for "from Paul's perspective Christians *must* and *can* lead a life that conforms to God's and not society's norms."[43] Perhaps it would do us all some good to read 1 Cor 5 again and contemplate the severe ridicule we cast upon our Lord when we tolerate these sins under the guise of (obscenely misunderstood) love and acceptance. "It needs to be said loudly, lovingly, and clearly that sexual loving apart from marriage is out of bounds, not because sex is bad, but because it is so good."[44]

What are the marks of a healthy, mature church? That question has multiple answers, but it isn't limited to doctrinal purity. It also includes excellence in our love for one another. Failing to give priority to brotherly love is a failure to restore NT Christianity. Too often, however, this doesn't always make the list of our top priorities. The modern church may chase growth by improving the worship service experience or hiring a more energetic, engaging preacher. "But, the Bible does not talk in

43. Green, *Thessalonians*, 201.

44. Demarest, *1, 2 Thessalonians*, 75.

those terms. It talks about something as mundane and down-to-earth as increasing brotherly love being the mark of reality."[45] As I was reflecting upon this, I came across a quote from Leon Morris. Since I am committed to the plea of "going back to the Bible" and restoring the NT church, his words are difficult to ignore. "Something that should give modern Christians much food for thought is the way in which the early church was characterized by love. 'Behold how these Christians love one another' [Tertullian, *Apology* 39] is hardly the comment that springs spontaneously to the lips of the detached observer nowadays. But if our manner of life was based on the New Testament picture, something like it would be inevitable. The characteristic Christian attitude, as we see there, is one of profound faith in God, a faith that spills out into all of life in the form of self-denying, self-giving love."[46] Maybe we should focus on loving one another just as much as we focus on being relevant or right.

---

45. Jackman, *Authentic Church*, 108.

46. Morris, *Thessalonians*, 127.

5

RETURN OF THE KING

The nondescript country road is easy to miss if you aren't looking for it. Only recently paved, it leads you up a hill and twists along a ridgeline to a clearing with a large oak tree. That tree stands solemn watch over a handful of headstones and the resting places of the dearly departed.

The Shuffledust cemetery in Prentiss County, Mississippi isn't much of a cemetery. I'd be surprised if more than a half-dozen souls rest there. It seems I always visit that place in the dead of winter, when leafless trees lift their naked branches to the sky in hopeful expectation of spring's warmth and hope. In this cemetery, buried under six feet of Mississippi soil, rests the body of my dad, awaiting the return of his King.

Whenever I visit my father's grave, I read 1 Thess 4:13–18 aloud. It helps that I know most of the passage by heart and can recite it from memory—my eyes always well up with tears, blurring the letters on the page. I am often alone in those moments, but I know that more than the trees and birds play audience to these words of Scripture.

I speak them aloud to Satan and his demons; those words resound with their death-sentence.

I speak them aloud to my Father and King; those words testify to his unparalleled glory.

I speak them aloud to myself; those words remind me to grieve as one with hope—hope that death is not the end.

The return of Jesus was a core component of Paul's teaching (e.g. Acts 17:31). In every chapter of 1–2 Thessalonians, there is at least one allusion to the Second Coming. But nowhere else in these letters (or in his other writings, for that matter) does the apostle communicate so clearly the events concerning Jesus' return. In fact, the final verses of 1 Thess 4 have brought tremendous comfort to countless saints through the ages. The promise of Christ's return, however, is not enough to guard us against Satan's schemes. In 1 Thess 5:1–11, Paul employs the promise of Jesus' return to urge the Thessalonians to remain watchful and faithful.

Christians are justified in their embarrassment and criticism of false prophets who claim that Jesus' return will occur on this day or that. In recent times, Harold Camping prognosticated that the end of all things would commence on May 21, 2011. In case you haven't figured it out, Camping was wrong. No one knows when Christ will return, which is precisely the reason Paul likens the event to a thief in the night. Even as we criticize these false prophets, however, we must not allow their failed prognostications to rob us of our vigilance. Camping and others like him are like the boy who cried, "Wolf!"—we eventually become so disenchanted and immune to predictions of Jesus' coming that we stop looking for it. We become like the five foolish virgins. "Always be ready, because you don't know the day or the hour the Son of Man will come" (Matt 25:13 NCV). How tragic when Christians no longer scan the clouds for his glorious return!

As you study this passage, may you be comforted by the great hope we have in Christ concerning the resurrection of the righteous. May you also learn to turn your glance upward, and often, to await the return of your King!

1 THESSALONIANS 4:13–18

We don't know the size of the Thesslonian church, but whatever its size, it had to have been a close-knit community. My dad labored in many small churches in Mississippi, and whenever there was a death, there was not a single member of that body who wasn't numb with grief. I imagine the Thessalonian church had recently experienced several deaths in their midst, and while they believed in the resurrection, they evidently were confused about the state of the dead when Christ returned. It is thought that the Thessalonians believed the dead at Christ's return would be at a disadvantage to the living[1] (cf. John 5:7), that they would be unable to share in the subsequent glory to the same degree.[2] This was certainly a popular notion in Jewish literature—"Understand therefore that those who are left [i.e. until the end] are more blessed than those who have died" (2 Esdras 13:24).

Paul opens this section with an emphatic phrase very common to his writings: "We do not want you to be uninformed" (e.g. Rom 1:13; 1 Cor 10:1; 2 Cor 1:8). He does not refer to the deceased as "the dead," but as those "asleep,"[3] a common euphemism for death in both the religious[4] and secular[5] literature of ancient times. As Wanamaker notes, "In both Greek writings and throughout the OT, with the exception of the Book of Daniel, the metaphor of sleep for death was used by those who had no real concept of afterlife."[6] On the other hand, Paul euphemistically uses "sleep" for "death" to highlight its temporary state.

---

1.   Marshall says the Greek term translated "precede" in 4:15 "contains the idea of doing something before somebody else and so of gaining an advantage over him," (*1 and 2 Thessalonians*, 127). Morris thinks it's possible that the Thessalonians believed "the deceased were under the wrath of God," (Morris, *Thessalonians*, 135; cf. Acts 5:1–11).

2.   "One may smile at such an erroneous idea now, but to the Thessalonians it was a major stumblingblock. This would, in their mistaken view, mean such things as possibly having those who were left behind forever separated from fellow Christian family members, being obliged to wander pointlessly about in some realm other than heaven or hell," (Woodson, *Perfecting Faith*, 76).

3.   Our English word *cemetery* derives from the Greek *koimōmenoi*, "sleeping ones."

4.   e.g. Gen 47:30; Deut 31:16; 1 Kgs 2:10; Job 14:12–13; Ps 13:3; Isa 43:17; Jer 51:39–40; John 11:11–13; Acts 13:36; 1 Cor 11:30.

5.   Homer, *Iliad* 11.241; Sophocles, *Electra* 509; Cicero, *On Old Age* 81.

6.   Wanamaker, *Thessalonians*, 167.

The ancient world had very little, if any, hope of life after death.[7] Leon Morris succinctly explains:

> Few things are more impressive in the contrast between early Christianity and the surrounding pagan systems than their attitudes in the face of death. Nowhere outside Christianity do we find at this period any widespread view of a worthwhile life beyond the grave. There are some statements on immortality in pagan literature. Undoubtedly some of the philosophers had an idea of a life beyond the grave. But they did not glory in it, and, in any case, theirs was the lofty view of the few. Nowhere did it penetrate to the beliefs of ordinary people.[8]

Many ancient authors bemoaned the finality of death. The Roman poet Catullus, for instance, said, "When once our brief light sets, there is one perpetual night through which we must sleep," (5.4–6). The Greek poet Theocritus exlaimed, "There is hope for those who are alive, but those who have died are without hope," (*Idyll* 4.42), and the Roman poet Lucretius lamented, "None ever wake again whom the cold pause of life hath overtaken." A letter from the second century A.D., discovered in Egypt, expresses the writer's condolences to a couple—Taonnophris and Philo—who had just lost their son. The writer, Irene, who had dealt with similar loss, wrote, "I sorrowed and wept over your dear departed one as I wept over Didymas, … but really, there is nothing one can do in the face of such things. So, please comfort each other," (*Papyrus Oxyrhynchus* 115).

The resignation to "this life is all there is" is tragically appalling; Morris describes it as "a pathetic little conclusion to a letter that reveals all too clearly that she has no comfort to give."[9] Even today, "Christian morticians

---

7. "Living hope as a fundamental religious attitude was unknown in Greek culture," (NIDNTT 2:239).

8. Morris, *Thessalonians*, 136.

9. Ibid., 137.

comment on the behavior of non-Christians at funerals: they exhibit the absence of hope."[10] These were the people the apostle had in mind when alluding to those "who have no hope" (cf. Eph 2:12; Heb 2:15).

The hope we have as Christians, the hope that death is not the end, is tied inextricably to the resurrection of Christ (cf. 1 Cor 6:14; 15:14, 23; 2 Cor 4:14). "It is by reason of Christ and His work, and by reason of that alone, that death's darkness is made beautiful, and death's grimness is softened down to this."[11] At the cross, Jesus absorbed every hideous reality of death so "that there is no horror in death for his people."[12] All assaults against the historicity of the resurrection are meant to rob Christians of their hope. No Easter equals no hope (Acts 26:23; Rom 8:11; 1 Cor 15:12–28; Col 1:18). "The Christian confidence is not the result of some philosophical speculation, nor the elaboration of a religious myth."[13] Rather, it is grounded in an event—in the darkness of Good Friday and the glory of that Sunday morning when the tomb was empty. Because we believe in the miracle of Jesus' resurrection, we also believe God will raise the dead through Jesus, for the Son is the first fruit of God's resurrecting power[14] (cf. 1 Cor 15:20).

What does Paul mean when he says "by a word from the Lord"? It could be a prophetic utterance inspired by Christ himself, perhaps a revelation from Jesus to Paul.[15] The Greek phrase translated "a word from the Lord" is very similar to the one used in the LXX for prophetic messages (e.g. Isa 1:10; Jer 1:4; Ezek 1:3). Both Paul and Silas were considered

10. Ward, *Commentary*, 103.

11. Alexander Maclaren, *Expositions of Holy Scripture: Philippians, Colossians, First and Second Thessalonians and First Timothy* (Grand Rapids: Baker, 1978), 196.

12. Morris, *Thessalonians*, 138.

13. Ibid.

14. McGarvey explains that the second half of 4:14 "does not here mean that Jesus will bring the disembodied spirits from *heaven* to the resurrection, but that God, who brought Jesus from the grave, will also bring from the *grave*, in conjunction with Jesus, all those who entered it with their lives spiritually united with Jesus," (*Thessalonians*, 20).

15. Larry W. Hurtado, *Lord Jesus Christ* (Grand Rapids: Eerdmans, 2003), 150–51.

prophets (Acts 13:1; 15:32). Alternatively, Paul could be referring to an actual statement Jesus made while on earth, one simply not recorded in the four gospels (cf. Acts 20:35). It could also be a restatement of Jesus' collective teachings on the subject; there is a great deal of support for this passage being based, whether directly or indirectly, on the Olivet Discourse (Matt 24; Mark 13; Luke 21).[16] If this is true, "then we may say that Jesus himself sets the pattern for the church's eschatology."[17]

Paul's description of Christ's return is ripe with imagery of a conquering king visiting his people. When he spoke of Jesus' "coming," he used the Greek noun *parousia*. The word meant the coming or revelation of an important person, e.g. a political leader or deity.[18] "Coming" or "presence" is the common defintion in the NT (cf. 1 Cor 16:17; 2 Cor 7:6; Phil 1:26; 2:12), and "both these ideas mingle when it is used of Jesus Christ's coming to be present with his people," (cf. Matt 24:3, 27, 37–39; 1 Cor 15:23; 2 Thess 2:1, 8).[19] The one NT occurrence of this word most similar to its usage in 1 Thess 4:15 is found in Acts 28:15. In this passage, a delegation of Christians from Rome came out to meet Paul and his companions at the Appian Forum in order to usher them into the city. What is more, the Thessalonians would recall the much ballyhooed visits by Pompey and Octavian to their city. Polybius describes the great pomp and circumstance of a VIP's *parousia* to a city (5.26.8), "and author after

---

16. cf. Comfort, "1 & 2 Thessalonians," 366; Witherington, *1 and 2 Thessalonians*, 136; David Wenham, "Paul and the Synoptic Apocalypse in *Gospel Perspectives*, vol. 2 (Sheffield: JSOT Press, 1981), 345–75; G. Henry Westerman, "The Sources of Paul's Teaching on the 2nd Coming of Christ in 1 and 2 Thessalonians," *JETS* 18 (1975): 105–13.

17. D. A. Carson, "Matthew" in *The Expositor's Bible Commentary*, vol. 8 (Grand Rapids: Zondervan, 1984), 489.

18. BDAG 780–81. "In view of the near-divinization of some rulers, there can be no hard-and-fast distinction drawn between these two uses of παρουσία in the Hellenistic-Roman world," (Bruce, *1 & 2 Thessalonians*, 57). Witherington notes the word's usage in reference to the Roman Emperor Hadrian and concludes that Paul is co-opting "the rhetoric of emperor worship" and applying it to Christ," (*1 and 2 Thessalonians*, 91).

19. Comfort, "1 & 2 Thessalonians," 362.

author described how not only certain officials but also all the population would file out of the city to meet the emperor in his parousia."[20]

According to the apostle, the return of Christ will be accompanied "with a cry of command," which Morris describes as "an authoritative utterance. ... It is the cry made by the ship's master to his rowers, or by a military officer to his soldiers, or by a hunter to his hounds, or by a charioteer to his horses. When used of military or naval personnel it was a battle cry."[21] Philo used the same word in reference to God's call/command to assemble the Jewish exiles scattered across the face of the earth (*Rewards* 117). This cry is directed to ~~the dead~~ the sleeping ones, those who await a reurrected life in the Kingdom (cf. John 5:25–29). We will also hear "the voice of an archangel"[22] and "the trumpet of God"[23] (cf. Matt 24:30–31; 1 Cor 15:52). In the OT, the trumpet was used to call assembly or send troops into battle (e.g. Num 10), so it is natural that the apostle links a trumpet blast with the gathering of God's people (cf. 1 Thess 4:17; 2 Thess 2:1). The OT also says that a trumpet blast would signal the day of the Lord (Isa 27:13; Joel 2:1; Zeph 1:16; Zech 9:14). Moreover, the Romans used trumpets to signal the coming (i.e. *parousia*) of a VIP. Paul, by using these specific terms, provides the image of heaven's army being dispatched as an administrator of God's justice (2 Thess 1:7; cf. Rev 19:14)

Three other terms in 1 Thess 4:17 enhance Paul's grand imagery of Jesus' return. The loud command will awaken the dead in Christ to resurrection, while the living will be "caught up," a Greek verb that "implies violent action, sometimes indeed to the benefit of its object," (e.g.

---

20. Green, *Thessalonians*, 227.

21. Morris, *Thessalonians*, 143; cf. BDAG 538.

22. Fee believes Paul had Michael the archangel in mind (*Thessalonians*, 177); Edwards agrees, noting that Michael is the only angel in Scripture designated as an "archangel" (*1 & 2 Thessalonians*, 134).

23. Bruce believes the angel's voice and the trumpet blast are the same thing (*1 & 2 Thessalonians*, 101). Fee argues that the angel and trumpet collectively constitute the "cry of command," (*Thessalonians*, 177).

Acts 8:39; 23:10; 2 Cor 12:2–3; Rev 12:5).[24] This might be a deliberate allusion to how Enoch (Gen 5:24) and Elijah (2 Kgs 2:11) were received into heaven. In an ironic twist, the term also appears in ancient grief literature—a bereaved father lamented that his son was "snatched away" before his time, "leaving me behind all alone" (Lucian, *On Funerals* 13). Paul, therefore, may be turning the phrase purposefully on its head just a bit; instead of being snatched from life to death, the living are snatched from a mortal life to eternal life.

The great reunion, we are told, will take place in the clouds[25] where we will "meet" the Lord. Like *parousia*, the Greek *apantēsis* ("meet") was a technical term for a delegation going out to welcome the *parousia* of a VIP. It appears in a parable of Jesus' return, one in which the ten virgins waited to "meet" the bridegroom (Matt 25:6). Cicero also used the term to describe the reception of Caesar on his victory tour through Italy in 49 B.C. (*To Atticus* 8.16.2; 16.11.6).[26] A perfect example of the connection between *apantēsis* and *parousia* is found in Josephus' account of the high priest in Jerusalem who goes out to "meet" the "coming" of Alexander the Great (*Antiquities* 11:26–28). In like manner, the above-mentioned Roman delegation arrived at the Appian Forum to "meet" the "coming" of Paul.[27]

For quite some time, scholars believed that the meaning of *apantēsis* demanded an interpretation of the resurrected and the living meeting the Lord in the air where they would escort him back to earth, just as a

24. Bruce, *1 & 2 Thessalonians*, 102.

25. Clouds are very closely tied to the divine presence throughout Scripture (Exod 13:21–22; 19:16; Lev 16:2; Num 9:15–22; 1 Kgs 8:10–12; 2 Chr 5:13–14; Neh 9:12; Ps 97:2; Isa 19:1; Dan 7:13; Matt 17:5; Acts 1:9, 11; 1 Cor 10:1–2; Rev 1:7; 14:14–15).

26. Malherbe points out that *apantēsis* was such a well-known word that Cicero didn't even bother translating it into Latin (*Thessalonians*, 277).

27. "This word in turn has had a considerable history of interpretation to the effect that it was a technical term for the ceremonial reception accorded distinguished persons at their 'coming' to a given city or province. But a recent investigation of the word has demonstrated that this is unlikely, and that all the other accoutrements of such ceremonial receptions are altogether missing from this passage," (Fee, *Thessalonians*, 180).

delegation would meet a VIP on the outskirts and escort him into the city.[28] Bruce, however, argues that "there is nothing in the word *apantēsis* or in this context which *demands* this interpretation."[29] Therefore, to use this passage to defend the doctrine of the Rapture is unwarranted.

That said, Paul in this passage doesn't seem as interested in *where* the Lord and his entourage go after the meeting since "we will be with the Lord forever."[30] This is the central hope of every Christian concerning the afterlife. What defines heaven is not the mansion, robe, or crown we often sing about; the glory of our final destination is not that we will live like Bill Gates with material wealth and possessions. Heaven, in its simplest form, is a place where we will be with God forever (Rev 21:3). Jesus himself promised, "If I go and prepare a place for you, I will come again and will take you to myself, that where I am you may be also" (John 14:3; cf. 17:24).

Paul ends the passage appropriately with an exhortation to the Thessalonians to use these words in order to comfort[31] one another. Irene's letter to Taonnophris and Philo concerning the death of their son concluded with, "Please comfort each other." There is no offer of hope, no comfort provided for those who live outside of Christ. They are without "hope and without God in the world" (Eph 2:12). On the other hand, the people of God have every hope and reason to be encouraged. In sharp and profound contrast to the hopelessness of the pagan world, God's people have a glorious future awaiting us on the opposite side of Jordan.

---

28. Marshall, *1 and 2 Thessalonians*, 131.

29. Bruce, *1 & 2 Thessalonians*, 103; cf. Michael R. Cosby, "Hellenistic Formal Receptions and Paul's Use of ΑΠΑΝΤΕΣΙΣ in 1 Thessalonians 4:17," *BBR* 4 (1994): 15–34. For a rebuttal, see Robert H. Gundry, "A Brief Note on 'Hellenistic Formal Receptions' and Paul's Use of ΑΠΑΝΤΕΣΙΣ in 1 Thessalonians 4:17," *BBR* 6 (1996): 39–41.

30. "Again we observe the gist of Paul's argument. There is no possibility that those who have died in Christ will ever be separated from Christ. They died 'through' him (14); they sleep 'in' him (16); they will rise 'with' him; and they will come 'with' him too (14). Christ and his people belong to each other inseparably and indissolubly," (Stott, *Message of Thessalonians*, 102–3).

31. Whiteley says "strengthen" here is a better translation than "comfort," (*Thessalonians*, 74).

1 THESSALONIANS 5:1-11

In the opening words of 1 Thess 5, Paul seems to switch to a new subject, but his remarks maintain focus on the Second Coming. However, while 4:13–18 dealt with the reality of such an event, as well as the comfort such a promise gives to God's people, the first eleven verses of 1 Thess 5 speak to the *when* of this event. Particular attention is paid both to its suddenness and unpredictability. Paul speaks of "the times and the seasons," terms that are individually distinctive,[32] but when combined, function as synonyms (cf. Dan 2:21; 7:12; Wisdom of Solomon 8:8; Acts 1:7).[33] The apostle's point is that the Thessalonians have no need to be instructed on *when* Jesus will return because no one can know (Mark 13:32). He goes on to say that knowing when is less important than being ready for "whenever."

There are many biblical passages that refer to "the day of the Lord." In the OT, this is a phrase with a dark and foreboding tradition. It was an elastic term referring to a day when God would act in judgment.

> See, the day of the LORD is coming —a cruel day, with wrath and fierce anger— to make the land desolate and destroy the sinners within it.
>
> Isa 13:9 NIV

> Alas for that day! For the day of the LORD is near; it will come like destruction from the Almighty.
>
> Joel 1:15 NIV

In the NT, however, the phrase is adapted to refer specifically to

---

32. "The word translated times has primary reference to indefinite and extended periods of time; the word translated seasons has reference to a definite and particular span of time (cf. Neh. 10:34; 13:31; Dan. 2:21)," (Kelcy, *Letters*, 104).

33. Wanamaker, *Thessalonians*, 178. He later adds that "the times and the seasons" and "the day of the Lord" collectively allude to Judgment Day.

Jesus' return[34] (cf. Rom 2:16; 1 Cor 1:8; 2 Cor 1:14; Phil 1:6, 10; 2 Tim 4:8; 2 Pet 3:12). It is also known as "the day of judgment" (1 John 4:17) and "the day of [God's] wrath" (Rom 2:5). Jesus himself called it "the last day" (John 6:39). Since Paul applies the term to the Second Coming, he obviously intends to invoke two concepts: destruction *and* deliverance. The advent of this day is likened to "a thief in the night."

Two thousand years removed from the apostle's time, we still associate the vast majority of burglaries and thefts with the night. In fact, we are so accustomed to this that we are more outraged when such activities occur "in broad daylight." Even the Greek playwright Euripides quipped, "Night is the time for thieves, daylight is the time for truth," (*Iphigenia in Taurus* 1025–26). Jesus himself used the image of a thief when he spoke of his return (Matt 24:43; Luke 12:39; 17:24–32; 21:34–36), and it appears again in later NT books (e.g. 2 Pet 3:10; Rev 3:3; 16:15).[35] Obviously, the thief metaphor highlights the need for vigilance.

In June 2010, I visited a hospital in Plano, TX to sit with a friend during his wife's cancer surgery. I parked my Jeep in the garage and made my way to the waiting room where I spent several hours. When I returned, I found a friendly warning from the parking garage security team that my vehicle was unsafe—I had left my Garmin GPS in plain sight on the dashboard, and such a valuable gadget often proved to be too tempting to petty thieves. I admit I didn't think too much about it as I drove away. I was both grateful for the warning and annoyed by it. I figured the parking garage was safe, and that the security guard had better things to do with his time. Five minutes later, I had forgotten all about it.

Two days later, my Jeep was burglarized overnight outside my apartment, and the GPS unit was stolen from its mount on the dashboard. If only I had heeded the warning…

---

34. "In practical terms, to speak about the day of the Lord is to speak of Christ's parousia," (Shogren, *1 & 2 Thessalonians*, 202).

35. "No truth seems to have been more clearly and fully taught than that the Son of man would come when not looked for by the world," (Lipscomb, *Commentary*, 63).

The thieves never gave me advance warning of their sinister plan. If they had, I would have made preparations: I might have taken my GPS off the dashboard and hidden it in the console or glove box. I might have kept watch during the night and caused a commotion when I spotted the thieves' arrival. I might have borrowed a friend's Rottweiler and let him sleep in the passenger seat. My point is that we often think of all the things we might have done to prevent theft, but *only when it's too late*. The time to make preparations for Christ's return is now, not after it has occurred.[36] How tragic it will be to stand before God at the Judgment, knowing we never prepared for the day of the Lord.

Second only to the confession that Jesus is Lord, the apostle's words in 1 Thess 5:3 may be the most politically treasonous and seditious in these two letters. While it was once thought that Paul was echoing OT prophets (Jer 6:14; Ezek 13:10)—and he may have been—there now seems to be more to his words than an echo of his ancestors. The Roman Empire prided itself in providing peace and security for its citizens. The terms ("security" less frequently than "peace") appeared on coins, monuments, official proclamations, and various propaganda pieces.[37] In the first century, the Roman historian Velleius Paterculus wrote about the day of Rome's establishment. "On that day there sprang up once more in parents the assurance of safety for their children, in husbands for the sanctity of marriage, in owners for the safety of their property, and in all men the assurance of safety, order, peace and tranquility," (*Compendium of Roman History* 2.103.5). Later, he added, "The Pax Augusta which has spread to the regions of the east and of the west, and to the bounds of the north and the south, preserves every corner of the world safe/secure from the fear of banditry" (2.126.3; cf. Josephus, *Antiquities* 14.247; Seneca, *On Mercy* 1.4.1–3; Tacitus, *Histories* 4.74).

"Peace and security" were bywords for the benefits made possible by

---

36. "The coming of the thief implies our loss, if he catches us asleep and unprepared. How fearful our loss if we are not prepared for the coming of the Lord," (McGarvey, *Thessalonians*, 23).

37. CNTUOT 881.

the Empire. The city of Thessalonica owed its peace and security, not to mention its prominent status, to the Romans. To question or oppose the claim would be akin to saying that the U.S. is nowhere near the greatest nation in the world, that *The Andy Griffith Show* was a terrible sitcom, or that the designated hitter is great for baseball. Paul, however, exposed the Empire's claim as impotent. When things seem to be great, "suddenly everything will fall apart. It's going to come as suddenly and inescapably as birth pangs to a pregnant woman" (5:3 Msg). Given that the American church invests a lot of faith in the U.S. military and the Bill of Rights, Paul's warning should convict us of so great an idolatry. Trust the government all you want, but know that such trust is utterly misplaced. The only thing that can save us from the greatest disaster the world will ever know is a radical, sincere confession of Jesus' lordship and preparation for his return.[38]

Jesus also used the imagery of labor pains to speak of his return (Matt 24:8; Mark 13:8), and while the metaphor was often used to express severe pain (e.g. Isa 13:8; Jer 6:24), it is used here to express both the unpredictability and inevitability of an event.[39] A pregnant woman can hardly predict the precise moment when her labor pains will begin, but she knows that she should expect them. Christians will not be caught off guard by Jesus' return, not because we know when it will occur, but because we are meant to remain ever vigilant, ever watchful, by living moral lives (cf. Mark 13:35, 37; Rev 16:15). Regarding thieves and pregnancies, Grant observes, "An important point about both of these illustrations is that you can make preparations. You can have a plan for a thief, such as a safe and a burglar alarm, and you can have a plan for the pregnancy, such as having your bags packed and friends on call. And that

---

38. "The reference here seems to be to those who place all of their eggs in this world's basket and live as though they could build the kingdom of God here on earth without His coming," (Demarest, *1, 2 Thessalonians,* 86).

39. Shogren points out that a woman dying in childbirth was so common in ancient times that a mother's life expectancy was in the 20s or 30s. "The woman's first contraction might therefore be the harbinger of death," (*1 & 2 Thessalonians,* 204).

leads to Paul's next point about how we should live."[40]

Employing language he will reuse in Rom 13:11–13, Paul urges his readers to continue living for the Lord until his return. In 1 Thess 5:6–7, Paul uses the metaphor of drunkenness.[41] Sobriety is associated with clear thinking and normalcy, thus drunkenness conversely expresses disorientation and deception. According to Paul, the lost experience these spiritual maladies because they don't love the truth (cf. 2 Thess 2:10–12). Not only are the lost unaware and unprepared for the return of Christ, but it also seems they wouldn't know how to prepare unless they received the Good News of Christ. The drunkenness metaphor is consistent with Paul's earlier allusion to sleep since both occur at night (cf. Acts 2:15). Even today, public drunkenness during the day is significantly less common, while drunkenness at night is more socially acceptable— you don't see a lot of DUI checkpoints at 10 am.

Paul continues to employ additional metaphors to communicate his point. This time, he turns to the images of day and night, darkness and light[42] (cf. Luke 16:8; John 12:35–36; Eph 5:8). In a world of artificial light, where activity doesn't come to a halt just because the sun has set, some of the power of Paul's metaphors may be lost. The very existence of light bulbs, however, testifies to how disorienting and disconcerting we consider physical darkness to be. Granted, I want it dark in the room when I'm asleep, but as soon as I awake, I'm searching for the light. No one wants to stumble or trip over obstacles hidden by the darkness. You do the same thing whenever you go in search of a drink of water, a midnight snack, or to use the toilet. You don't have to be a teetotaler to appreciate the drunkenness metaphor either—I'm not exactly "sober," alert, or vigilant before my morning coffee!

We are children of the day, so we can survive the world's darkness

---

40. James H. Grant, Jr., *1 & 2 Thessalonians* (Wheaton, IL: Crossway, 2011), 141.

41. Comfort says that "sleep" refers to moral indifference, while "drunkenness" refers to lack of moral restraint ("1 & 2 Thessalonians," 364).

42. cf. Shogren, *1 & 2 Thessalonians*, 205–6.

by putting on the armor Paul describes in 1 Thess 5:8. It's commonly thought that he is echoing Isa 59:17 here: "He put on righteousness as his breastplate, and the helmet of salvation on his head" (NIV). Both in Isaiah and Eph 6:13–17, faith is described as a shield and righteousness the breastplate; in all three passages, salvation is the helmet. Instead of getting bogged down in any possible distinction between them[43] (I doubt Paul intended to make one), the greater point is that God dons armor in Isa 59 to wage war against evil, just as Christians are meant to wear this same armor in order "to withstand in the evil day" (Eph 6:13). To put it another way, faith, hope, and salvation (the latter possibly invoking God's love) collectively guard us from a dark, drunken, and disoriented world. No wonder, then, that Paul so affectionately remembered these traits in his prayers for the Thessalonians.

Christians must remain vigilant and wear this armor because "God has not destined us for wrath, but to obtain salvation through our Lord Jesus Christ." What a glorious affirmation! It is not the Father's will that his children experience his righteous anger and terror, thus he made it possible for us to be saved from it through the death, burial, and resurrection of Christ (cf. Rom 5:8–9). Those outside of Christ, those who never confessed him as Lord and obeyed his gospel, "will not escape"[44] this wrath (cf. Amos 9:2–3; Rev 6:15–16).

In this, Paul once again swings the discussion back to where it truly belongs. Despite all of our vigilance, watchfulness, preparation, sobriety, and armor—both the living and dead in Christ[45] will rejoice at the return

---

43. If a distinction is to be made, consider that a shield and breastplate serve the same function—they protect a soldier's core. Trust in God and love for him and one another protect our spiritual core, our heart, from wickedness and evil. Salvation's helmet protects our head from Satan's lies.

44. Paul uses a double negative in 1 Thess 5:3, emphasizing the impossibility of the lost escaping God's wrath.

45. In 1 Thess 5:10, Paul gives the awake/asleep metaphor the same meaning as in 4:13–18. This is an important distinction; we shouldn't mistakenly assume that he intends "awake" and "asleep" to represent the righteous/wicked or prepared/unprepared. "It is ludicrous to

of our King because of what God has done. "If we live, we live for the Lord; and if we die, we die for the Lord. So, whether we live or die, we belong to the Lord" (Rom 14:8 NIV). Is it God's work or man's that matters most? Paul's answer would be, "Yes." Both are necessary, but God should receive all the credit because our work is ultimately by God's grace! Imagine how wondrous that day will be when we can sing God's praises and give credit to our King forever and ever and ever!

What a day, glorious day, that will be.

---

suppose that the writers mean, 'Whether you live like sons of light or like sons of darkness, it will make little difference: you will be all right in the end,'" (Bruce, *1 & 2 Thessalonians*, 114).

TALKING POINTS

O nly the most astute readers of the Greek text will notice Paul's subtle shift from the present participle (*koimōmenōn*) in 4:13 to an aorist participle (*koimēthentas*) in 4:14. In doing so, Paul stresses that having a glorious share in the return of our King depends on whether we died in Christ; whether we belonged to him when we "fell asleep."[46] I often heard my dad conclude his sermons with these words: "I don't know your family doctor, but if I were to ask him or her, I would probably be told that you will eventually die. What will happen? If you are lucky, the preacher will say a few nice things about you, but they then will take you to the cemetery, dig a six-foot hole in the ground, bury you, return to the church building or somebody's house, and eat potato salad and fried chicken. You will be gone and the only thing that will matter is whether you died in a right relationship with God. Only you can decide whether you will die in Christ."[47] After burying my dad, my family returned to the church building to share a meal. When I walked in, I noticed potato salad and fried chicken resting on the table. I couldn't help but smile. Yes, many fine things had been said about my father at his funeral. Yes, he had now been buried in a six-foot hole. Yes, he was gone. Everyone dies. But he had died in Christ, and in Christ, death has no victory (John 11:25).

I t is not wrong to grieve; if it were, Jesus would have sinned at Lazarus' tomb (John 11:35). But the attitude with which we grieve can provide a powerful witness to the world concerning the hope of the gospel. In a 2005 interview, Katie Couric remarked, "I really envy those who have a steadfast, unwavering faith, because I think it's probably so comforting and helpful during difficult times." Couric lost her husband, only 42 years

46. Wanamaker, *Thessalonians*, 169.

47. "For Christians death is no longer that adversary whom no person can resist, that tyrant who brings all worthwhile existence to a horribly final end. Death has been overcome by the risen Lord, and that has transformed the whole situation for those who are in him," (Morris, *Thessalonians*, 136).

old, to colon cancer in 1998; her sister passed away in 2002.[48] It seems she witnessed, somewhere, hope in the face of death, and it motivated her to become more spiritual. "I'm very interested in exploring a more spiritual side of me, and I'm in the process of doing that, both formally and informally," she concluded. The hope Christians have concerning death is a beacon of light to the world, and what we believe should shape how we behave. As we grieve the loss of our loved ones, let us allow Christ to be magnified in our grief so that more will live in earnest anticipation of his return and that great homecoming around the throne of God.

D id Paul believe Jesus would return in his lifetime? Scholars point to the "we" language of 1 Thess 4:13–17 for an answer in the affirmative, only to turn around and scorn the apostle under the assumption that he should have somehow known better. Such rhetoric could have been employed to arouse in Paul's readers an eagerness for the Second Coming, as well as a subtle reminder that it *could in fact come* in their lifetimes.[49] David Lipscomb believed no conclusion at all could be drawn concerning whether Paul expected to be alive or dead at Christ's return.[50] Lipscomb's conclusion may be drawn from the fact that Paul seems to believe he will be alive at the Second Coming in some passages (e.g. 1 Cor 15:52), but dead in others (e.g. 1 Cor 6:14; 2 Cor 1:8; 4:14). Shogren offers a valid point—since Paul's life was in constant danger (cf. 2 Cor 11:23–27), "one should wonder how such a man could expect to see any future event, let alone Christ's return."[51] In the end, Witherington offers the most balanced response: "[Paul] does not know that he will *not* be alive when Jesus returns, and so the only category in which he can

---

48. Cable Neuhaus, "Whatever Katie Wants," *AARP* (November–December 2005).

49. Calvin, *1, 2 Thessalonians*, 49. "Paul's imagery of the thief implies a denial of knowing with that sort of precision," (Witherington, *1 and 2 Thessalonians*, 134).

50. Lipscomb, *Commentary*, 57.

51. Shogren, *1 & 2 Thessalonians*, 184.

logically place himself and the Christians he writes to here is the 'living.'"[52]

I've heard some very insensitive things said to the bereaved. These words are often spoken out of an irrational compulsion to say *something, anything*—and not to comfort the mourner as much as the speaker himself. To a new widow, I once heard a woman remark, "I know just how you feel; my dog died last week." To parents who were facing the burial of their child, another said, "God must have decided that his heavenly garden wasn't as it should be, so he plucked your child as a flower to bring his garden greater beauty." I often counsel people that, if they feel the need to say something at the funeral home, "I'm sorry" and "I love you" are all that is necessary. As time goes by, other words may become necessary, but in the beginning, keep it simple. Paul commanded us to comfort one another with his words from 1 Thess 4:13–17. In light of this, J. W. Shepherd reminds us, "Words, we often feel, are vain and worthless; they make no difference in the pressure of grief. Of our own words that is true; but those we have been considering are not our own words, but the words of the Lord. His words are living and powerful. Heaven and earth may pass away, but they cannot pass. Let us comfort one another with these precious words."[53]

When it comes to peace and security, some of us put the cart before the horse. Gaventa points out that we deadbolt our doors, put flood lights outside, and install alarm systems with motion detectors and off-site monitoring in order to feel safe in our own homes. We value security in our jobs, in our relationships, in our finances, and in our national defense. "By contrast, the security Paul commends cannot be won or increased or even seen by human eyes. As the world measures 'peace and security,' the

52. Witherington, *1 and 2 Thessalonians*, 134; cf. Robert H. Stein, "Did Paul's Theology Develop? (1 Thess. 4:13–18)" in *Difficult Passages in the Epistles* (Grand Rapids: Baker, 1988), 82–88.

53. Lipscomb, *Commentary*, 62.

gospel has nothing to offer."[54] Gaventa is right. Christ's message can never guarantee that your retirement, your job, or even your personal safety will never be at risk—one might even argue that the gospel places all these things at greater risk when we obey it. We live under the delusion that we can achieve peace and security in this life, but we cannot. The gospel compels us to realize that the only real security lies in submitting to the lordship of Christ, because the trust we deposit in him is guaranteed. "I know whom I have believed, and am convinced that he is able to guard what I have entrusted to him until that day" (2 Tim 1:12 NIV).

54. Gaventa, *Thessalonians*, 75.

6

FINAL INSTRUCTIONS

When I was very young, my dad wrote letters to my mom, sister, and I just in case he were to die suddenly and unexpectedly. He then stowed them in the lock box kept under my parents' bed, where they remained for nearly fifteen years. In March 2002, he threw away those letters and wrote new ones in preparation for his trip to India, a country not entirely safe to visit a mere six months after the nightmare of 9/11. Dad's mission trip came and went without incident, and everyone forgot about those new "goodbye" letters...

Until two and a half years later when he passed away suddenly and unexpectedly.

The evening after we buried dad, mom retrieved the letters and handed them out. I vividly remember reading mine for the first time. I still have that letter; it is among my most prized possessions. In it, my dad didn't say anything too profound, but then that wasn't his intent. Mostly, he told me he loved me and was proud of me, but he also left some parting instructions. These instructions didn't necessarily have to do with anything painfully amiss in my life (though there was a warning about driving too fast; I had gotten my first speeding ticket the day before he left for India). Rather, the instructions represented what dad considered to be simple, yet important things that I absolutely must not lose sight of after he was dead and gone. Two commands particularly stand out in my memory:

Always honor my mom and never abandon the Lord and his church.

At the close of his first letter to the Thessalonians, Paul passed on several final exhortations. These instructions should not imply that the Thessalonians struggled with these particular issues.[1] Rather, this passage was Paul's way of passing on a few final notes he considered important. The themes Paul touches on here are varied and seemingly unconnected, but each one falls under the umbrella of God's will for us.[2] If his readers practiced these things, Paul's prayer—"May God sanctify you completely" (1 Thess 5:23)—would be answered.

1 THESSALONIANS 5:12–13

Every era of history has faced some sort of a leadership crisis, but none more than ours. On a national level, the President and Congress never seem to agree on what is best for the country. In Washington D.C. itself, party building is more important than engaging in effective leadership. In our homes, we have a crisis of leadership as well. There are more single-mothers than ever before because fathers are not discharging their God-given responsibility to lead their home. It was a sad sign when, in December 2012, "a dad" made the top 10 list of things kids asked for most for Christmas.[3]

Regrettably, there is also a leadership crisis in our churches. We expect our preachers to have a top-notch education in Scripture and theology, but when it comes to elders or shepherds, the bar is set ridiculously lower.

---

1. This passage is ripe with present imperatives in the Greek, which were typically used for listing general rules for life not specific to any specific situation (Daniel B. Wallace, *Greek Grammar Beyond the Basics* [Grand Rapids: Zondervan, 1996], 721).

2. "Because many of the specific exhortations are conventional, readers may find themselves rushing through this passage to finish the letter. Resisting that temptation is important since many of the letter's central themes (such as relationships within the community, the Parousia, the faithfulness of God) come together once again in these final lines," (Gaventa, *Thessalonians*, 79).

3. Hannah Furness, "A 'dad' is tenth most popular Christmas list request for children," *London Telegraph*, December 24, 2012.

Other times, it seems "ability to make a company profitable" trumps "ability to make a family spiritual" when it came to qualifications to be an elder. I'm not targeting elders alone, either. Ministers and deacons are also to blame for the weak display of leadership in churches around the country.

Strong leadership may be absent because of sin: e.g. arrogance, pride, selfishness, and greed. Other sins exist as well: the desire to be well liked and popular, the unwillingness to commit to a course of action lest they make a bad decision, or a reluctance to seek outside counsel. All of these fallacies have their roots in sin.

It is human nature to regard leadership with a measure of disdain and suspicion, but Americans all too often pretend it is our birthright to do so. Against this stands Paul's command to respect ("appreciate," NASU) and esteem our spiritual leaders[4] (although all leaders deserve the same from us, cf. 1 Tim 2:1–2; 1 Pet 2:17). Regrettably, some churches do not follow this admonition as they should. Paul would condemn those members who "get mad and leave" over hurt feelings, or who sue leaders over an unpopular decision. The apostle's words merit our somber reflection, not only because they constitute a command, but also because love and respect do more to transform a leader into all he should be, while disdain and suspicion perpetuate the negative stereotype.

Included in these verses is a reminder that leaders should "labor among" the congregation, rather than lord over them with a heavy hand. They are to be esteemed "because of their work,"[5] but it is not their status that entitles them to respect and love.[6] It is their diligence in getting

---

4. Paul seems to mention three groups: "those who labor among you," those who "are over you," and those who "admonish you." But in the Greek, one definite article is used, meaning Paul is actually delineating three tasks for leaders, instead of having three different groups in mind.

5. Time and again in the NT, "labor" was often used to describe the work of ministry (e.g. 1 Cor 3:8; 15:58; 2 Cor 6:5; 11:23; Gal 4:11; Phil 2:16; Col 1:29; 1 Tim 4:10; 5:17). "It is not a question of personal prestige; it is the task which makes a man great and it is the service he is doing which is his badge of honour," (Barclay, Letters, 206).

6. "It is perhaps significant that they [leaders] are given no title here [e.g. 'bishops' or 'elders']; their work was more important than a title," (Morris, Thessalonians, 165).

their hands dirty, in setting a compelling example in good works (cf. Tit 2:7) that identifies them as ideal leaders. Given a church culture that sometimes chooses elders because they were successful business leaders (and therefore among the wealthier members of a congregation), this should give us pause. Paul strongly suggests that we choose our leaders from a pool of those *already* doing the work of the church (as opposed to the dicey practice of appointing leaders and then giving them a job). In Thessalonica, the church's leaders were most likely those already functioning as supporters of the congregations (e.g. Jason, Acts 17:5–9).

Paul warns that leaders only have authority over a congregation "in the Lord." "Church leaders are not autonomous sovereigns but represent Jesus' authority. They are commissioned by Christ to carry out their oversight of the flock according to his will and not their own."[7] While this precludes leaders from being bullies, it also requires them to "admonish" those in need of instruction. Admonishing does not necessitate provoking or embittering someone (cf. 1 Cor 4:14). These leaders are meant to function "as guardians of the community by urging its members to avoid improper behavior and guiding them into conduct appropriate to the gospel."[8]

Paul does not speak here of a naïve trust in leadership, but rather a healthy appreciation. It is just as wrong for a church to be ungrateful for her leaders as it is to be openly hostile towards them. In some ways, preachers have a corner on the encouragement market, however small it may be in a given congregation. Meanwhile, shepherds often go weeks, months, or years without receiving a meaningful expression of respect and loving esteem, even though they have the most thankless job in a congregation.[9] If every member properly understood the high expectations the NT places on shepherds, sincere love and appreciation would well up in their

---

7.   Beale, *1–2 Thessalonians*, 161.

8.   Victor Paul Furnish, *1 Thessalonians, 2 Thessalonians* (Nashville: Abingdon, 2007), 115.

9.   The Greek word translated "labor" in 5:12 is often used of strenuous physical exertion (cf. 1 Cor 4:12; 1 Thess 2:9). Metaphorically, the word expresses the great challenge church leaders face as they discharge their duties in a way that honors the Chief Shepherd.

hearts toward their leaders.

The final exhortation in these two verses, "Be at peace among yourselves," can be easily fulfilled. Members must learn to appreciate and respect one another, rather than taking each another for granted. Such a command is found many times in Paul's letters (Rom 12:18; 14:19; 2 Cor 13:11; Eph 4:3; Col 3:15; 2 Tim 2:22), which is why Edwards concludes, "Every Christian is obliged to do everything within his power to promote peace in the congregation of which he is a member."[10]

1 THESSALONIANS 5:14–15

In every congregation, there are "problem" people. On second thought, to call them problems isn't very nice. So let's go with "challenging people." A minister quickly learns that faces and names change from place to place, but personalities often remain essentially the same. Beginning with 5:14, Paul addresses the entire congregation (not just the leaders, as some mistakenly assume) in order to discuss three types of challenging people. Paul functions like a doctor; to each individual case, he prescribes a different approach, but patience is the right medicine for every situation.

First, he calls upon the church collectively to "admonish the idle," though the Greek *ataktoi* would be better translated as "unruly" (cf. NASU, NKJV). The word was often used of soldiers who were out of line or who had abandoned their post and gone AWOL. Green says the word was used in Berea to refer to those who refused to obey the rules of the gymnasium,[11] and thus described someone who was disruptive, undisciplined, and disobedient (cf. 3 Maccabees 1:19; Josephus, *Wars* 2.517; *Antiquities* 15.152). There are Greek words signifying those who were idle or lazy (e.g. *argoi, apraktoi*), but Paul did not use these here. "Unruly" would certainly encompass the idle, but the apostle had in mind a broader category in this particular verse. Among early Christian writers,

---

10. Edwards, *1 & 2 Thessalonians*, 182.

11. Green, *Thessalonians*, 253.

"unruly" became an umbrella term for all who acted contrary to God's revealed will. Philo described unruly behavior as "seditious, faithless, disorderly, impious, unholy, unsettled, unstable" (*Sacrifices* 32).

Paul says we must admonish the unruly. To admonish meant "to counsel about avoidance or cessation of an improper course of conduct."[12] In the past, admonishment was sometimes done in an abusive way, but there is no room for humiliation or a punitive spirit. That said, "One cannot stand idly by and observe fellow Christians walking in forbidden ways and say or do nothing. There is risk in such warning, but there is more importantly the responsibility."[13] In an age where anti-bullying campaigns are so popular, I fear that the church might confuse admonishment with bullying and adopt a conflict-avoidance policy. It requires wisdom, discernment, and patience to understand who needs admonishment. It is a tough job, but the souls of the unruly depend on it!

We are also called to "encourage the fainthearted" (cf. "discouraged," HCSB; "timid," NIV). "Fainthearted" is a difficult term to translate as it occurs nowhere else in the NT, and only a small handful of times in the LXX (e.g. Exod 6:9; Prov 18:14; Isa 35:4). It literally means "small spirit/soul" and was used by Aristotle to describe those shy or modest persons who suffered from feelings of inadequacy (*Nicomachean Ethics* 4.3.3–7). Ward defines the fainthearted as "those whose spirit is all but broken and who are on the verge of 'giving up.'"[14] Paul could be referring to those discouraged by the persecution facing the Thessalonian church; the Greek term is used in the LXX, after all, to describe a lack of endurance in the face of trials (cf. Num 21:4; Isa 25:5; 54:6; 57:15).[15] Regardless of why these individuals were discouraged, Paul knew they needed support.

I know some Christians who always seem to fear the worst and are a

---

12. BDAG 679.

13. Woodson, *Perfecting Faith*, 93.

14. Ward, *Commentary*, 115.

15. Beale, *1–2 Thessalonians*, 165.

little too eager to hit life's panic button at the slightest feeling of distress. "These are the quitters in the church family. They always look on the dark side of things and give up when the going is tough."[16] It can be draining and tedious to minister to these individuals; instead of encouragement, I want to admonish them to grow a backbone or stop being a Debbie Downer. Obviously, this is not the medicine the Great Physician wants us to administer. He calls us to encourage the discouraged! If we fail this charge, they may be overwhelmed by Satan's schemes.

The final category of challenging people is "the weak." It is virtually impossible to discern whether Paul means the physically (cf. 1 Pet 3:7) or spiritually weak (cf. Jas 5:14); I'm inclined to think Paul had both in mind. It's easier (and, sadly, often the case) for the weak to slip through the cracks. Months or years can lapse before someone questions, "Whatever happened to so and so?" Their attendance and participation in the life of the church may have dropped off because of pressures from family or work, or because of internal feelings of guilt, such as not fitting in, etc. These people need our help! "The Christian community should make a deliberate attempt to grapple him [the weak] to the Church in such a way that he cannot escape. It should forge bonds of fellowship and persuasion to hold on to the man who is likely to stray away."[17]

To all these admonitions, Paul adds the call to his readers to remain patient. He does not employ the common Greek term for patience, *hypomonē*, but rather *makrothymeite*, which has the addend nuance of "long tempered." It "carries the sense of 'suffering long' with regard to someone else. It is therefore the appropriate word to use regarding human relationships, while *hypomonē* moves in the direction of enduring difficult situations."[18] In the second century A.D., Ignatius encouraged Polycarp to "bear with all people, even as the Lord bears with you; endure all in love,

---

16. Wiersbe, *Be Ready*, 113–14.

17. Barclay, *Letters*, 239.

18. Fee, *Thessalonians*, 211.

just as you now do ... If you love [only the] good disciples, it is no credit to you; rather with gentleness bring the more troublesome ones into submission," (1.2; 2.1).

Dealing with challenging people requires tremendous long-suffering, but it is what God expects of us. Is this the status quo? Is this how we treat challenging people? Most every church "offers ample evidence that Paul's instructions constitute a profound challenge to the way things are. Sometimes we are not patient; we are merely indifferent."[19] Long-suffering is a virtue we should cultivate if for no other reason than it is a virtue of God (Exod 34:6; Joel 2:13; Rom 9:22). God is patient with his people, hoping it leads to their salvation (Rom 2:4; 1 Tim 1:16; 1 Pet 3:20; 2 Pet 3:9, 15); in the same way, our patience with challenging people may lead them deeper into a trusting relationship with Christ.[20] Our patience with one another is an act of love (1 Cor 13:4; Eph 4:2) and proof of the Spirit's work in us (Gal 5:22).

It is so tempting to seek revenge, to mete out our own justice. The apostle, however, firmly warns us against it (cf. Luke 6:27–36; Rom 12:17). This is a particularly relevant command to a church that had struggled with persecution and injustice. Our natural instinct is to strike back when disrespected or when others make life difficult for us; it is a survival instinct in its basest form. Vengeance, however, has no place in the Christian life.

If I'm honest, I could have done without Paul's final command in 1 Thess 5:15. I can find it within myself not to seek revenge against those who have wronged me, but to expect me "to do good...to everyone" seems too much to ask. It is compounded by Paul's use of "pursue," which can also mean "persecute." The apostle may be suggesting that the

---

19. Gaventa, *Thessalonians*, 83.

20. "The disorderly are not to be too hastily considered apostates, nor are the fainthearted to be regarded as cowards, nor the weak called backsliders, nor are any to be hastily cast out; but the church, being slow to condemn, is to bear with offenders, and seek to reclaim them," (McGarvey, *Thessalonians*, 25).

Thessalonians pursue good deeds for all people with the same tenacity that Paul had exhibited in persecuting the church (cf. Phil 3:6).[21] Few could be accused of being "fanatical" about doing good deeds. All the same, this is the Christian's call,[22] and Paul is not speaking of "good" in the abstract, but that which is beneficial to others, even our enemies.[23] Whiteley captures the importance of this command:

> The fact that [the Thessalonians] were far more sharply demarcated from the world than is normal in modern times led the pagans to suspect them, and to accuse them of crimes for which there was no possible basis. In a "war situation" each side almost inevitably exaggerates the faults of the other. It is likely that the Christians also were less than fair to the pagans. It was probably under such circumstances as these that Paul urged the Christians of Thessalonica to seek the good of *all*, that is the pagans and the Jews.[24]

1 THESSALONIANS 5:16-18

The final phrase of 5:18 actually encompasses the three commands of 5:16–18. In other words, joy, prayer, and thanksgiving are collectively "the will of God in Christ Jesus for you." The phrase "in Christ Jesus" could not be more important[25] because joy, prayer, and gratitude are only

---

21. Ward, *Commentary*, 115.

22. "It is important to notice a significant consequence of Paul's command to do good to everyone (friend and foe alike): It hinders the development of a dualistic perspective—the tendency to view everyone outside our group or aligned against us as evil (or at least on the side of evil). Instead, it reminds us of God's love, care, and concern for everyone. It forces us to expand our perspective toward that of God's, rather than reduce his to the limitations of ours," (Holmes, *1 and 2 Thessalonians*, 194).

23. Bruce, *1 & 2 Thessalonians*, 124.

24. Whiteley, *Thessalonians*, 83.

25. "Paul's statement that God's people are in *Christ Jesus* should remind them that they are to see all things through the lens of Christ and not from their own vantage point. As a

possible for the Christian because of Jesus. He came to bring us joy (John 10:10), to make it possible for us to approach the Father in prayer (1 Tim 2:5; Heb 4:14–16), and to make it possible for his people to be thankful (rather than despondent) in all circumstances (cf. Phil 4:11–13).

The shortest verse in the Greek NT is not John 11:35, but 1 Thess 5:16—"Rejoice always." Biblical, godly joy is a product, not of circumstances, but of the gospel. Thus there is a fundamental difference between happiness and joy. It is also important to note that rejoicing is the expression of joy, so we are not simply discussing a feeling or emotion. Put another way, to rejoice is to make a conscious decision to express joy,[26] regardless of one's circumstances. For Christians, no matter what else is happening, we have every reason to rejoice if we are in Christ, in whom exists every spiritual blessing (Eph 1:3).[27]

Recall who writes these words in 5:16, and to whom they were written. Paul was at this time facing significant challenges in Corinth, and the Thessalonians were under fire from local authorities, as well as their own neighbors and family members. The letter to Philippi, often known as the "Epistle of Joy," was written from a Roman prison. All the same, the letter mentions "joy" or "rejoice" an average of every eighteen verses. "The apostles never encourage believers to deny that adversity brings sadness and grief (see 4.13; 1 Pet. 1.6; Rom. 12.15), but they recognize that in the midst of the most agonizing situations the presence of God through his Spirit can infuse the soul with hope and the heart with joy."[28] In that sense, our capacity for authentic, biblical joy may rest on how much we trust God.

---

consequence, they will experience peace," (Beale, *1–2 Thessalonians*, 171).

26. "The very use of the imperative forces us to regard rejoicing, praying, and giving thanks as things other than feelings," (Demarest, *1, 2 Thessalonians*, 95).

27. "If our Christian experience does not lead to joy, we do well to ask whether it is genuine," (Marshall, *1 and 2 Thessalonians*, 154).

28. Green, *Thessalonians*, 258. "To rejoice always is to see the hand of God in whatever is happening and to remain certain of God's future salvation. Without such conviction joy would not be possible in the face of affliction, suffering, and death," (Wanamaker, *Thessalonians*, 200).

I'm struck by the embarrassing realization that I show more joy or happiness over worldly things than I do spiritual. If the Dallas Cowboys or Alabama Crimson Tide have recently won a big game, I'm quite joyful (but let's not talk about the recent performance of the Dallas Cowboys, or the result of the 2013 Iron Bowl. It's still too painful). I find joy in a large bag of M&Ms, a hot cup of coffee, or when my wife makes my favorite dessert. In the grander scheme of things, however, none of these delights matter nearly as much as what God has done for us in Christ. Christians can "rejoice always" because "setback" isn't in God's vocabulary (cf. Rom 8:31). Heaven doesn't have terrible, horrible, no good, very bad days— Good Friday stands as proof of this. For some of us, a good place to start would be to express the same joy over the gospel as we do when our favorite team wins. The next time the Cowboys win a playoff game, I'll show you what such joy should look like!

One cannot read through the whole of Paul's letters without realizing that prayer was as natural to the apostle as breathing.[29] Jesus encouraged us "always to pray and not lose heart" (Luke 18:1). The command, "Pray without ceasing," is better translated as "pray constantly" (HCSB) or "continually" (NIV). We talk often about wanting to restore the NT pattern, but some have a long way to go before they have restored the NT church's example of being fervent in prayer. The greatest weapon in the hands of an oppressed people is prayer. If it is not our first and regular response when challenged or persecuted, then we betray the fact that we do not feel a strong dependence on the Lord.

To "pray constantly" means to maintain a constant attitude and demeanor of prayer, an on-going conversation with the Lord.[30] Throughout any given day, my wife and I carry on a conversation via phone calls, text messages, emails, etc. A few years ago, she traveled full-time with her job,

---

29. Morris; *Thessalonians*, 173.

30. "To 'pray without ceasing' does not mean that every other activity must be dropped for the sake of prayer but that every activity must be carried on in a spirit of prayer which is the spontaneous outcome of a sense of God's presence," (Bruce, *1 & 2 Thessalonians*, 127).

but technology enabled us to feel as if we were still connected, though physically separated by thousands of miles. I think the same concept is at play in Paul's command to "pray constantly." Although we cannot see him, we are drawn powerfully to God's heart by getting on our knees.

My dad, who had to endure a lot of terrible things in his brief life, often told me, "You can either be bitter or better." In addition to being a prayerful people, Christians need to be a grateful people. The godless may be ungrateful (Rom 1:21), but God's people must overflow with thankfulness (Col 2:7; cf. Eph 5:4, 20; Col 3:15, 17; 4:2). We cannot give this point any less consideration than it deserves. In 1 Thess 4:3, the apostle says that God's will for us is to practice sexual purity and fidelity. Here, it is joy, prayer, and gratitude. None of these are any less important to our heavenly Father than the others.

It's important to note that Paul says to express gratitude "in everything" (HCSB), not "for everything." I have no obligation to be thankful that my dad died at 44 instead of 84. I can, however, still give thanks that he was an amazing father, a godly influence, a faithful minister of the gospel, etc. You don't have to be thankful for your terrible circumstances, but you must give thanks in your circumstances, lest you undermine the joy God wants you to experience in the midst of unspeakable pain.[31] For the Thessalonians, giving thanks regularly would realign their attitude in the face of mounting persecution, for if they did not, they would be overwhelmed by Satan's schemes.

1 THESSALONIANS 5:19–22

The five commands of 5:19–22 are intimately connected, but if at

---

31. "No matter what the circumstances (persecution, sickness, etc.) the Christian ought to be able to give thanks to God, not of course for the difficult circumstances but for his salvation through Christ, and when he is able to do this then he also is strengthened to endure what is difficult," (Best, *Thessalonians*, 236). Beale draws excellent ties between prayer and thanksgiving. Prayer gives way to gratitude because we 1.) are reminded of past answered prayers, 2.) contemplate the nature of God and his grace to us, and 3.) confess sin and are thereby reminded of what Jesus did for us through the gospel. "To the extent that we have a prayerful attitude we will have a thankful one," (Beale, *1–2 Thessalonians*, 169).

the outset you feel disoriented by what Paul discusses, know that you are not alone. "Do not quench the Spirit" is rather vague as to its precise meaning. Is this a reference to the miraculous gifts of the Spirit (cf. 1 Cor 12:4–11), or to the non-miraculous work of the Spirit to bear fruit in the Christian's life (cf. Gal 5:22–23)? Regardless, to quench means to put out or stifle, as if putting out a fire (Matt 12:20; 25:8; Mark 9:48; Heb 11:34). Ward likens the phrase to our idiom "pouring cold water" on something (cf. "throwing a wet blanket").

In our day, quenching the Spirit can occur when we refuse to apply the Word to our lives because of laziness or rebellion, or when we neglect reading Scripture altogether. We quench the Spirit when we pretend that Scripture's claims should be subjected to cultural norms or political correctness. As Spurgeon summed it up, "Do not quench him by neglect, much less by open opposition."[32]

Despising prophecy is a narrower form of quenching the Spirit. Although miraculous prophecy has ceased in our day (1 Cor 13:8), it is still possible for the Word of God to be despised: Bibles are forgotten in the pew or the car instead of being read voraciously throughout the week. Passages are cherry-picked and valued as more important than other Scriptures in order to suit personal ambition. Christians complain when the sermon goes 10–15 minutes longer because it interrupts their Sunday schedule. Members nitpick the message for grammatical faux pas or bristle if and when their toes are stepped on.[33] In 2013, Barna Research found that 88% of survey respondents owned a Bible, and that the average household had 4.4 Bibles; 57% of those who said they read the Bible at all only did so four times or less a year, while 26% read it four or more times

---

32. C. H. Spurgeon, *The Metropolitan Tabernacle Pulpit Sermons*, vol. 55 (London: Passmore, 1909), 516.

33. "Despise not anyone who speaks in God's name. He may speak with blunders of grammar—forget them; if he be correct in his teaching of divine truth, if he speaks to your heart, if he warns you, if he warns under the Spirit of God, never despise him," (C. H. Spurgeon, *The Metropolitan Tabernacle Pulpit Sermons*, vol. 62 [London: Passmore, 1916], 131).

a week.[34] The gift of prophecy may no longer exist, but that doesn't mean prophecy can no longer be despised.

Instead of swallowing everything (especially prophecy and other works of the Spirit) hook, line, and sinker, the apostle encouraged his readers to "Test everything" (cf. Deut 18:21–22; 1 Cor 12:10; 14:29; 1 John 4:1–6). This command bears a striking resemblance in the Greek to a saying of Jesus not recorded in the gospels, but widely attested in early Christian literature: "Be approved moneychangers," our Lord purportedly said.[35] The illustration is one of bankers requiring the ability to spot counterfeit versus authentic coins. Christians must learn to discern truth from error, good from bad. We cannot always trust the source. If you think this is much ado about nothing, I should tell you that the Thessalonians later believed error about the Second Coming because they gave undue credibility to a prophecy or forged letter from Paul (2 Thess 2:2).

Paul does not go into detail as to *how* the Thessalonians are to test everything, but "presumably the standard was the accepted tradition of Christian teaching already passed on to the church."[36] Another factor was the moral behavior of the speaker. A document from the early-second century A.D. known as the Didache (meaning "teaching") contains practical instructions for the early church. It instructed, "Not everyone who speaks in the spirit is a prophet, but only if he exhibits the Lord's ways. By his conduct, therefore, will the false prophet and the prophet be

---

34. Caleb Bell, "Americans Love The Bible But Don't Read It Much, Poll Shows," *Huffington Post*, http://www.huffingtonpost.com/2013/04/04/americans-love-the-bible-but-dont-read-it-much_n_3018425.html, (accessed December 14, 2013).

35. Joachim Jeremias, *Unknown Sayings of Jesus*, trans. Reginald H. Fuller (New York: Macmillan, 1957): 89–93. Altogether, Jeremias references 37 quotes and 20 allusions to this saying, "in which the consensus with regard to the wording and interpretation is remarkable," (89). Morris concludes, "We should probably regard this as a genuine saying of Jesus," (*Thessalonians*, 178, n. 68).

36. Marshall, *1 and 2 Thessalonians*, 159; cf. Holmes, *1 and 2 Thessalonians*, 189, 197–98. "Even today, in finding the difference between what is true and what is false, there is no substitute for searching the word of the Lord," (Coffman, *Commentary*, 71).

recognized. ... If any prophet teaches the truth, yet does not practice what he teaches, he is a false prophet" (11:8–10). This sentiment conforms to Jesus' warning: "Watch out for false prophets... by their fruit you will recognize them" (Matt 7:15, 20 NIV). Another factor was whether something was edifying, encouraging, or comforting to the church (1 Cor 14:3; cf. Phil 4:8). In this is a stern condemnation of those preachers who spiritually and habitually abuse their audiences under the despicable guise of "contending for the faith" or some other mantra. There are times where criticism and condemnation are necessary, but such must be done in love and cannot become the normal pattern.

The irony is that elsewhere, Paul claimed the Spirit enables Christians to discern these matters (1 Cor 12:10). Therefore, there is every reason for Christians to test everything, whether it comes from Joel Osteen, Oprah Winfrey, or their favorite preacher. "Test everything," whether it is on the Internet or in a book by your favorite author. "Test everything," whether it seems suspicious or completely trustworthy. Once something has passed the test, we are to hold on to it tightly.

The translators of the KJV unknowingly instigated a massive misunderstanding of 5:22 by translating it as "abstain from all appearance of evil." In other words, if something even *looks* evil, Christians should avoid it, no matter how innocent it is intrinsically. While the Greek term can have this meaning (e.g. Luke 9:29; 2 Cor 5:7), this is *not* what Paul intended in this passage.[37] As Spurgeon put it, "By which is not meant as some read it, 'from everything that somebody likes to say looks like evil.' This would be to mar the Christian liberty."[38] If I avoided everything that anyone might possibly view as "evil," it would be an exhaustive and wasteful enterprise. The Greek term translated "appearance" (KJV) or "form" (ESV) more specifically means "the various kind or species or type

---

37. "Paul is not speaking of 'what appears to be wrong' but 'evil, which shows its face in many ways,'" (Shogren, *1 & 2 Thessalonians*, 227).

38. C. H. Spurgeon, *The Metropolitan Tabernacle Pulpit Sermons*, vol. 62 (London: Passmore, 1916), 132.

of something." "Paul thus enjoins his readers to abstain from everything that is actually evil."[39]

1 THESSALONIANS 5:23–28

The language of Paul's closing in his letters echoes the themes he has mentioned throughout it; in other words, the closing "functions as a hermeneutical spotlight, drawing our attention to what Paul considers to be one of the major themes of that letter."[40] For all his final instructions, Paul knew sanctification remained God's work, so his closing prayer here was a request for God to continue this process and bring it to completion (cf. Ps 138:8; 1 Cor 1:8–9; Phil 1:6). "The believer can thus be sure not only of his present acceptance by God (Rom. 5:1), but also of his 'final perseverance'; although Paul would insist that those who persevere are those who put their trust in God and do not turn away from him."[41]

A lot of ink has been used on distinguishing "spirit and soul and body" (5:23). It is best, however, to interpret the phrase as only an expression of the whole person.[42] In other words, Paul prays, "May your whole person be kept blameless," which "is another way of expressing the desire for their complete sanctification."[43] God wants to save and set apart our whole person. He desired all his brethren to be ready, blameless, and complete at the Second Coming (cf. Col 1:28). The motivation for holy, righteous living is the return of our King; how sad to miss that great event because we did not live and long for him!

---

39. Malherbe, *Thessalonians*, 334.

40. Jeffrey A. D. Weima, "The Pauline Letter Closings: Analysis and Hermeneutical Significance," *BBR* 5 (1995): 177–98.

41. Marshall, *1 and 2 Thessalonians*, 164.

42. "Together these terms refer to the whole person, and the fact that God must sanctify, transform, and preserve the whole person before and at the parousia, for Paul is envisioning persons in resurrection bodies, who therefore will indeed be perfect and blameless living sacrifices offered up to the Lord Jesus," (Witherington, *1 and 2 Thessalonians*, 173).

43. Bruce, *1 & 2 Thessalonians*, 129.

It was certain that the Thessalonians would be found ready as long as they remained devoted to the Lord our God, for he will do all that he has promised. He has destined those in Christ for eternal salvation, so we have nothing to fear. "The One who called you is completely dependable. If he said it, he'll do it!" (5:24 Msg).[44] Or, as Augustine prayed, "Give me the grace to do as you command, and command me to do as you will," (*Confessions* 10.29).

Having revealed his prayer for the Thessalonians, Paul then solicits their prayers for himself and his companions (cf. Rom 15:30; 2 Cor 1:11; Eph 6:18; Phil 1:19; Col 4:3; 2 Thess 3:1).[45] Whether tension or friction exists in a congregation, it is imperative that church members pray for one another. Pray for the members. Pray for the ministers. Pray for the leaders. This is Paul's request. As a friend recently remarked to me, "It's difficult not to love, respect, and appreciate those for whom you pray regularly."

In Western culture, it is standard practice to greet others with a handshake, whereas in the East, it is still common to kiss one's cheek. Paul calls this "a holy kiss," which clearly means he does not have something sensuous or erotic in mind, i.e. a kiss on the lips.[46] If this is the only conclusion we draw on this verse, we have engaged in a colossal exercise of missing the point.

Among the Gentiles in ancient times, the kiss of greeting was reserved almost exclusively for close family members (cf. Gen 27:26–27; 29:11, 13;

---

44. "The most significant thing about the church is that it is the company of people held in existence and maintained in truth not by human will or effort but by the sheer faithfulness of God," (Wright, *Paul for Everyone*, 134).

45. "There is also the thought that through prayer the churches share in the work of mission; those who cannot go on mission themselves can share in the work by praying for missionaries. It is clear that Paul felt himself very dependent upon the prayers of his friends," (Marshall, *1 and 2 Thessalonians*, 164).

46. Fee, *Thessalonians*, 232, n. 91; Witherington, *1 and 2 Thessalonians*, 176. By the fourth century, opposite-sex kisses were prohibited in the church (*Apostolic Constitutions* 2.57.17). That this practice is often misunderstood today is illustrated by Spurgeon's statement, "To attempt to import it to the West would be not only absurd, but wicked," (C. H. Spurgeon, *The Metropolitan Tabernacle Pulpit Sermons*, vol. 62 (London: Passmore, 1916), 132.

Exod 4:27; 18:7; 2 Sam 14:33; Luke 15:20). One can imagine the scandal created when this became the standard greeting in the church[47] (Rom 16:16; 1 Cor 16:20; 2 Cor 13:12; 1 Pet 5:14). The church was a family, the household of God[48] (1 Tim 3:15), so the early Christians adopted a traditional family greeting in order to express this newfound community of love and acceptance. In the time of Justin Martyr (c. A.D. 150), the kiss of greeting was practiced during observance of the Lord's Supper, after the prayer and before the passing of bread and wine (*Apology* 65.2).[49] "In Paul's world a kiss was also a sign and means of reconciliation and so served as a deterrent to factionalism,"[50] (cf. Gen 33:4; 45:15; Luke 15:20). Our phrase, "kiss and make up," preserves an element of this idea. That's why it is so important to note that Paul's command (and to call it anything else is irresponsible) was to kiss "all God's people" (NIV). If every Christian at Thessalonica went out of the way to show affection to the other members, any divisions that previously existed would eventually evaporate.

Paul's command to greet with a kiss is followed with a solemn charge to publicly read the letter to the whole church.[51] Why did Paul put them "under oath before the Lord"?[52] Few of the Thessalonians would have

---

47. "What would be most remarkable about this expression of mutual Christian love within the believing community is the radical crossing of social boundary lines that would have been involved, not only between Jew and Gentile but also between rich and poor, slave and free," (Fee, *Thessalonians*, 232; cf. Beale, *1–2 Thessalonians*, 177).

48. "For members of a congregation to kiss one another was not simply a show of affection; it was the affirmation that the church is the true family," (Shogren, *1 & 2 Thessalonians*, 234).

49. William Klassen, "The Sacred Kiss in the New Testament: An Example of Social Boundary Lines," *NTS* (1993): 122–35.

50. Witherington, *1 and 2 Thessalonians*, 176; cf. Jeffrey A. D. Weima, *Neglected Endings* (Sheffield: JSOT Press, 1994), 111–14.

51. "The public reading would also bind the apostle again with this young church. The letter stood in the place of the apostle and was representative of his presence and authority," (Green, *Thessalonians*, 272).

52. Bruce calls this "an appeal to those addressed to act in this matter as responsible to the Lord himself," (*1 & 2 Thessalonians*, 135).

been literate,[53] but there seems to have been more to Paul's command than this, since he does not always give this injunction in his letters. Bruce suggests that the unruly or disorderly were most in need of hearing the letter's contents, and they were equally unlikely to be present in the assembly (cf. Heb 10:25). "The responsible leaders of the church should therefore see to it that they [i.e. the unruly] were made acquainted with its contents."[54] Paul wanted everyone to hear his letter read, particularly those who needed it the most.

---

53. Comfort, "1 & 2 Thessalonians," 380. He estimates that only 10% of the first-century population could read.

54. Bruce, 1 & 2 Thessalonians, 135. For an extended list of explanations as to why Paul gave this command, see Malherbe, Thessalonians, 344).

TALKING POINTS

Preachers have, for the most part, figured out the appreciation/ gratitude aspect of church life. We know that if we stand at the back door after a worship service, members can't leave without shaking our hand and saying something nice about the sermon, even if they slept right through it. Shepherds, on the other hand, often perform a thankless job. They may go months or years without any meaningful expression of gratitude for the tough role they fill in the church. Paul encouraged the Thessalonians to love and respect their leaders because of their endless work. This suggests that the church would benefit from greater teaching on the role of elders and the NT vision of their responsibilities. "When we understand what leaders actually do, love should well up in our hearts for them because of their sacrificial work on our behalf."[55]

A requirement for one of my college courses was to read through a book of the NT before each class period. The class only met twice a week, and since that meant more required reading before a class period, I would go to the library just before and read through the assigned book. It was probably the first time in my life I had read through whole books of the Bible in one sitting. I will always be grateful for those assignments. In my congregation, we often read through a book of the Bible publicly in our worship on a Sunday night in lieu of a sermon. I do so because I take seriously Paul's charge to Timothy to give himself to the public reading of Scripture (1 Tim 4:13), but also his charge to the Thessalonians in 1 Thess 5:27. This is but one suggestion on how to give Scripture greater prominence in the life of the church. We must be people of the Book, or face certain destruction (Hos 4:6). Christians must become fluent in the Word so that they are better equipped to test everything and reject the bad while clinging to the good.

---

55. Beale, *1–2 Thessalonians*, 162.

G rowing up, we never lived very close to relatives because my dad
preached in several different congregations, so the church became
"like family." Some members became so close that they were adopted as
uncles/aunts. We celebrated birthdays, holidays, and other life events
with them. We ate in their homes often, and they in ours. Our shared faith
provided us many, many opportunities to celebrate the glory of being a
part of God's family. Family is more than blood relatives; it's those with
whom you celebrate the fellowship of Jesus. It bothers me that so many
commentators go out of their way to explain why "Greet all the brothers
with a holy kiss" isn't an example we should emulate today. I'm not
advocating that we restore the practice per se, as much as the principle.
"What is important is that the members of the church should have some
way of expressing visibly and concretely the love which they have for
one another as fellow-members of the body of Christ. The manner of
expression may vary in different cultures; but it is doubtful whether doing
nothing at all, as modern western Christians tend to do, really fulfills the
spirit of the injunction."[56] If the church is anything, it is the family of God
(1 Tim 3:15), a group of individuals from every walk of life bound together
by a common faith in the Lord Jesus Christ. In a world where prejudice
remains alive and well, the church must become the very definition of an
unconditionally loving community. In short, it must be a family.

56. Marshall, *1 and 2 Thessalonians*, 165; cf. Holmes, *1 and 2 Thessalonians*, 203.

7

PROPERTY OF GOD

I had a rather annoying and embarrassing habit as a kid. It's not something I'm proud of, nor am I all that eager to tell you about it. But this is the seventh chapter of this book, and that makes us close friends, so here goes: I used to go around placing labels on random objects, marking them as my personal property. The labels read, "This is the property of Michael." I put them on my toys, my books, and several kitchen appliances. I was proud of my things and wanted everyone to know to whom they belonged.

Eventually, I turned my labeling tendencies towards creating real art. When I was about eleven, I became quite prolific in sketches and watercolor paintings and would initial all of my artwork with a unique signature. The final stem of the "M" would descend into the first stem of the "W," with a "C" in the middle. Artists sign their work so that no one can deny who created the masterpiece. Even with unsigned artwork, experts can point to certain characteristics that identify the creator. It's easy to discern a Rembrandt from a Norman Rockwell sketch, and a Thomas Kinkade painting would never be mistaken for a van Gogh or Monet. Alexander Maclaren said, "The artist is known by his work. You stand in front of some great picture, or you listen to some great symphony, or you read some great book, and you say, 'This is the glory of Raphael, Beethoven, Shakespeare.' Christ points to His saints, and He says, 'Behold My handiwork! Ye are my witnesses. This is what I can do.'"[1]

_____

1. Maclaren, *Expositions*, 251.

What is the identifying mark of God's masterpieces? What is it that sets Christians apart as creations of his handiwork? In 2 Thess 1, Paul establishes faithful endurance in the face of affliction as a strong trademark of God's masterpieces; our ability to suffer and persevere is his signature on our souls. This is a disconcerting concept for many modern Christians. In American church culture, we thank God for our religious freedoms, even though the Son of God said the persecuted are blessed, and that persecution is cause for rejoicing (Matt 5:10–12). Can you imagine a Christian publicly praying, "Lord, thank you that we are *not* pure in heart"? I'm not scorning our freedoms, nor am I particularly eager to be persecuted. The American church is averse to persecution, but we shouldn't be (cf. Jas 1:2) since it is a distinguishing mark of God's true people. As Green so elegantly puts it, "The Christian paradigm is always the cross."[2]

In the opening verses of 2 Thessalonians, Paul offered encouragement to a church still enduring regular affliction. He assured them that persecution authenticated their faith, instead of exposing it as a fraud. He also spoke of the day when the Christians there would be vindicated, the day when our King would return for his people and punish those who torment us. The question we must ask ourselves in light of this is, "Where will I spend eternity?" The answer depends on whether we allow ourselves to become God's property in this life.

2 THESSALONIANS 1:1–4

This second letter to the Thessalonians opens in an almost identical fashion to the first. The three authors are again named—Paul, Silvanus (i.e. Silas), and Timothy. It is addressed to the Thessalonian church, which exists "in God our Father and the Lord Jesus Christ." The greeting of grace and peace is also extended, just as in the previous epistle (cf. 1 Thess 1:1).

Paul also opens this letter with a prayer of thanksgiving for the

---

2. Green, *Thessalonians*, 285.

Thessalonians and their spiritual growth.[3] Their faith was "growing abundantly" and their love for one another was "increasing." Specifically, their faith was growing on the inside, like a mighty tree.[4] "The faith of Paul's readers had been a major concern for him since his abrupt departure from them, and was one of the reasons why he had sent Timothy to them, to strengthen them in their faith (1 Thess 3:2, 5)."[5] How overwhelming it must have been for the apostle to hear that they were standing firm! Increasing[6] love for one another among the Thessalonians was the very thing Paul had requested in 1 Thess 4:9–10—God had answered his prayer!

The way in which the Thessalonians were growing in their faith and love drove Paul to boast about them to other churches. The Thessalonians were enduring "persecutions" and "afflictions"[7] when the apostle penned this letter, but they had not forgotten how to love one another or to trust the Lord. As was the case in 1 Thess 1:8, Paul believed these Christians to be a perfect example of what it meant to live and long for the Lord.

The apostle's encouragement in this passage is important. As new Christians, I imagine many of the Thessalonians were wondering, "Are we doing this right? Is the heartache worth it?" Imagine you try a new diet plan everyone is raving about. All your friends seem to be losing weight and feeling great, so you give it a go. Dedicated, you maintain the required strict diet, exercise like crazy, and after six weeks, all your hard work has ...

---

3. Paul begins a long sentence in 2 Thess 1:3 that continues through 1:10. Although English translations break up the sentence into smaller sections to better communicate what Paul is saying, we must not forget that everything in these verses is a united concept.

4. "The obvious illustration is the mustard seed (Matt. 13:31 f.; Luke 13:19) which grows into a tree, though we need not limit ourselves to the luxuriant growth of vegetation. When faith is growing in the way in which Paul saw it grow, there is an increase in strength. Faith—or the believing man—can stand more strain," (Ward, *Commentary*, 137).

5. Malherbe, *Thessalonians*, 384.

6. "This synonym too has the sense of profuse or even overabundant growth," (Shogren, *1 & 2 Thessalonians*, 244).

7. Marshall argues that these terms are used synonymously (cf. Mark 4:17; Rom 8:35) for rhetorical effect (*1 and 2 Thessalonians*, 172).

Failed. You lost no weight, but rather gained three pounds.

This gives us a very small glimpse into the emotional toll these persecutions exacted from the Thessalonian Christians. Imagine the mental anguish caused by the cognitive dissonance of trying to believe in a just and loving God, yet seeing evidence all around you that life is not fair.[8] No wonder, then, that Paul went out of his way to brag on them, to compliment their growth, and to assure them that their trials were proof that they truly belonged to God.

2 THESSALONIANS 1:5–10

Paul's claim in 1:5, that their endurance in trial was proof of God's righteous judgment, is both arresting and confusing. Their persecutions and afflictions were making them "worthy of the kingdom of God" (cf. Acts 5:41; 14:22). Some believe we are made worthy through suffering, in that we pay for our sins in this life, rather than the one to come.[9] I reject this notion based on Paul's clear assertions that those in Christ are under no condemnation whatsoever (Rom 8:1). In 2 Thess 1, he explains that being made worthy through suffering means "the evidencing of true faith in God by steadfastness when one is tempted to abandon faith."[10] There is also a sense of God's election of the Thessalonian church for salvation being validated by their faithful endurance. Elsewhere in his writings, Paul interprets standing firm against opposition as solid proof of salvation (cf. Phil 1:27–28).

I don't know about you, but that idea unsettles me. How can suffering be evidence of God's justice? Isn't the reality of suffering and evil a common argument against God's goodness, not to mention his very existence? I'm more comfortable believing in retribution theology,

---

8. Shogren, 1 & 2 Thessalonians, 247.

9. "In this theological framework it is viewed somewhat paradoxically as a sign of acceptance by God insofar as he offers through it an opportunity for his elect to receive in this age the punishment for their few sins, thus preserving the full measure of their reward in the age to come," (Jouette M. Bassler, "The Enigmatic Sign: 2 Thessalonians 1:5," CBQ 46 [1984]: 502).

10. Marshall, 1 and 2 Thessalonians, 173.

a sort of Christianized karma, the belief that bad things happen to bad people and good things happen to good people. The theory is as old as the book of Job, wherein the ancient patriarch's three friends collectively tried to convince him that his suffering was a result of his sin (e.g. Job 4–5, 8, 11, 15, 22). Even in Jesus' day, when the Lord encountered a blind man, his disciples assumed that either the blind man or his parents had sinned. Jesus' response was as unexpected as Paul's—"This came about so that God's works might be displayed in him" (John 9:3 HCSB). Suffering sometimes occurs because of our sinful choices, but it also happens in order to refine our faith and make us worthy of God's Kingdom.

In Rom 12:17–21, Paul encourages his readers to abstain from vengeance in order to leave place for the Lord's wrath. He adopts a similar (yet distinct) approach in 2 Thess 1:6 by giving the Thessalonians a broader scope of things. Our thirst for vengeance is shortsighted, he says, because it cannot appreciate the punishment God will bring to those who have hurt us. Civil government is a more capable administrator of justice and punishment than are victims. In this passage, Paul rightfully presents God as the ultimate just and righteous Judge. It is God who has sworn to afflict the "afflicters" (Isa 66:6). Christians must wait until the last day to see all wrongs righted, but we can be sure that God will act, for he has sworn to do so (Rom 2:6–8; 12:19; 2 Cor 5:10; Col 3:25). On that last day when God acts on the behalf of all his people, he will bring us more than "rest" (1:7 HCSB, NKJV); he will bring "relief" from our suffering.

When our King returns from heaven,[11] his "mighty angels" will accompany him (cf. Zech 14:5; Matt 13:41–43; 24:31; 25:31; Mark 13:26–27; 1 Thess 3:13; Rev 19:17), a phrase better understood as "the angels who are the ministers of his power."[12] Angels were present when the Law was given at Sinai (Deut 33:2; Acts 7:53; Gal 3:19), and they

11. "He comes from heaven, a phrase which does not merely indicate his origin but also stresses his authority. He comes from the dwelling place of God with the authority of God to execute judgment and recompense," (Marshall, *1 and 2 Thessalonians*, 176).

12. Fee, *Thessalonians*, 256.

likewise will be present at the Judgment (Luke 12:8). At Jesus' coming, they will function as "the executors of the Lord's judicial power."[13]

Throughout Scripture, fire is often representative of the divine presence since it communicates brightness, glory, and purity (e.g. Exod 3:2; 19:18; Deut 33:2; Dan 7:9–10). Thus, Christ's coming will be "in flaming fire." This metaphor was also used for the fierce, destructive, punishing wrath of God.[14] In fact, Paul may be invoking the words of Isaiah—"See, the LORD is coming with fire, and his chariots are like a whirlwind; he will bring down his anger with fury, and his rebuke with flames of fire" (66:15 NIV). Notice that Paul, in this passage, applies to Jesus a statement originally made about God.

The "vengeance" Jesus will bring is not like the petty vindictiveness of which we mere humans are sometimes guilty. In fact, the Greek word Paul used to convey this concept is not burdened by any of the baggage of the English word. As N. T. Wright explains, "God is not a petty or arbitrary tyrant, who throws his political opponents into jail simply for being on the wrong side. God is the living and loving creator, who must either judge the world or stand accused of injustice, of letting wickedness triumph."[15] It cannot be gainsaid that God is committed to the integrity of his righteousness and justice.

It's commonly thought that Paul had two different groups in mind when he spoke of "those who do not know God" and "those who do not obey the gospel." Marshall argues that the first group refers to the Gentiles (cf. Ps 79:6; Jer 10:25; 1 Cor 1:21; Gal 4:8–9; 1 Thess 4:5), and the second to the Jews[16] (cf. Isa 66:4; Acts 7:39; Rom 10:16). The problem is that the distinctions could easily be reversed, with the Jews being "those who do not know God" (cf. Jer 4:22; 9:3–6; Hos 5:4; John 8:55) and the Gentiles

13. Green, *Thessalonians*, 289.

14. Num 11:1; Ps 97:3; Isa 26:11; 66:15–16; Jer 4:4; 17:4; Ezek 21:31; Nah 1:6; Zeph 1:18; 3:8.

15. Wright, *Paul for Everyone*, 143.

16. Marshall, *1 and 2 Thessalonians*, 178.

being those who reject the gospel (cf. Rom 11:30–32). That being the case, it's better to interpret the second phrase as clarifying the first; it is a willful rejection, not just simple ignorance, which combines both Jews and Gentiles into one group.[17] "Therefore, it is best to see Paul as describing a single group consisting of all those who will receive divine retribution for their failure to know God and obey the gospel,"[18] (cf. Rom 2:9–11).

What Paul means, then, is that "eternal destiny is bound inextricably with one's response to the gospel of Christ," (cf. John 14:6; Acts 4:12).[19] Some people may think they will get into heaven if God wakes up on the right side of the bed that morning. The litmus test, however, is much simpler. "It should be observed that this final separation implements the choice already made by men (John 3:19–21). ... This fearful doom is God's Amen to their persistent secular prayers."[20]

The fate of those who have rejected Jesus and his gospel will be eternal punishment and destruction—what Malherbe calls "everlasting ruin."[21] Paul did not believe in the concept of annihilation, the belief that the soul is destroyed and ceases to exist at some point in eternity, rather than suffering conscious, eternal torment. The Greek adjective *aiōnios* is used by Jesus in Matt 25:46 to describe both "eternal punishment" and "eternal life." Claiming that hell's torment is not eternal, but heaven's glory is, seems ridiculous when one realizes that the same word is used for both. Scholars like Marshall doubt that Paul believed in annihilationism,[22] though he also notes that the discussion is pointless since, "What mattered for Paul

17. Holmes, *1 and 2 Thessalonians*, 213.

18. CNTUOT 885.

19. Green, *Thessalonians*, 295; cf. Acts 6:7; Rom 1:5; 6:17; 10:16; 15:18; 16:26; Heb 5:9; 1 Pet 1:2, 14, 22.

20. Ward, *Commentary*, 144, 147.

21. Malherbe, *Thessalonians*, 402.

22. He argues that 1.) Both Jesus and Paul believed hell to be eternal, conscious torment, 2.) Jewish literature accepted the reality of eternal punishment, and 3.) Being separated from the Lord for eternity matters little if one is not aware of it (Marshall, *1 and 2 Thessalonians*, 179).

was the fact that their destruction was synonymous with exclusion from the presence of the Lord."[23]

The biblical image of hell is one too terrible to contemplate. There is weeping (Matt 8:12), gloomy darkness (2 Pet 2:4), unquenchable fire, and the worm that endlessly devours the damned (Mark 9:48). Imagine that we knew nothing of hell apart from Paul's statement in 2 Thess 1:9. Its terror would still be too ghastly to contemplate. Hell is a place where one is separated from "the presence of the Lord and from the glory of his might." It is a place where God is not (Matt 7:23; 25:41; Rev 22:15). Take away the flames, the unending, conscious torment, and gnashing teeth—it remains a place of unimaginable pain, particularly for those who spent a lifetime longing to be with the Lord (cf. 1 Thess 4:17). "The horror of this end will not be so much the pain which may accompany it as the tragedy which is inherent in it, namely that human beings made by God, like God, and for God, should spend eternity without God, irrevocably banished from his presence."[24] More than anything else, I want to spend forever giving thanks to the One who gave me love and life, joy and peace. In hell, this will be impossible.

At this point, it would help to take a step back and recall the original audience and cultural setting of Paul's words. The apostle and his companions had come to Thessalonica with a message that confessed Jesus of Nazareth to be the Lord of all. Such an acknowledgment was in direct contradiction to the claim of the Roman Empire that Caesar was lord (Acts 17:7). This radical claim caused many problems for Paul and, subsequently, for the Thessalonians. Even now, the church there continued to be persecuted for their belief in a King other than the emperor. Imagine how their collective hearts must have soared at the thought of their King returning in unparalleled glory "to be glorified in his saints, and to be

---

23. Ibid. "Paul's definition of 'destruction' (cf. 1 Thess. 5:3) here is precisely the opposite of his definition elsewhere of salvation as being with the Lord always (1 Thess. 4:17) and sharing in God's glory (Rom. 8:17–18, 30; 2 Cor. 4:17; Phil. 3:21)," (Holmes, *1 and 2 Thessalonians*, 214).

24. Stott, *Message of Thessalonians*, 154.

marveled at among all who have believed" (1:10). The reception their neighbors often gave to political VIPs would be of little comparison to the one the Thessalonian Christians would give the Lord Jesus Christ.[25]

At first glance, "glorified in his saints" and "marveled at" by believers seems to be two ways of saying the same thing. There is actually another way of interpreting the "in" from the first phrase—that "Christ's glorification takes place in the presence of believers,"[26] (cf. John 17:10). In other words, at the Second Coming, Christ's glory will be reflected in the hearts of his saints so that it creates the most brilliant of lights. Imagine a bright spotlight surrounded on all sides by an infinite number of mirrors; only then can you have a faint idea of what it will be like when Jesus is glorified in his saints at his coming.

Another way of illustrating this is to think of an artist and his masterpieces. No one beholds the Mona Lisa and congratulates the painting itself on a job well done. We instead stand in awe of da Vinci's skill with a brush. Authors are praised for their writing, musicians for their majestic melodies, and Cheesecake Factory for their otherworldly accomplishments with cheesecake. We praise the master for the masterpiece![27] In the same way, we will glorify our Master at his return for the masterpieces borne of his heart and hands. His property will bring him praise! What does it mean to marvel at our returning King? Tim Keller explains:

> The word marvel means more than just admire. The word marvel means to have your expectations exceeded. It means to have your desires exceeded. It means to have your imagination exceeded. Thomas Watson, the

---

25. "The Lord Jesus, who was so despised in Thessalonica, will come with great authority and judicial power, accompanied by the those who will aid in the execution of divine judgment," (Green, *Thessalonians*, 289).

26. CNTUOT 885.

27. "The wisdom and skill of the artist are displayed in the quality of his masterpiece, which wins him the admiration of those who appreciate it," (Bruce, *1 & 2 Thessalonians*, 153).

Puritan, says marveling means the overflow of your mind and heart. More than I ever dared ask or think. We're going to see that.[28]

Who is it that will see their desires exceed their wildest expectations and overflow their minds and hearts?

They who "believed"; poor, trembling, struggling, fainting souls, that here on earth, in the midst of many doubts and temptations, clasped His hand; and howsoever tremulously, yet truly put their trust in Him, these are they in whom He shall "be wondered at." The simple act of faith knits us to the Lord.[29]

When our King returns, our tears will become triumph, and our pain will become praise. His coming will be even more glorious than we ever anticipated. We will experience relief and be with the Lord forever.

What a day, glorious day, that will be.

2 THESSALONIANS 1:11-12

Paul knew the end of the story. More specifically, he knew the goal of the Christian life—to be among those who marvel at the return of the King. "To this end," he says, "we always pray for you." What does he pray? He beseeches God to make them worthy of their call and empower their desires to do good and act out their faith.[30] The apostle is clear in saying that the power of God is just as crucial to our faithfulness as our

---

28. Timothy J. Keller, "Marveling at Jesus," in *The Timothy Keller Sermon Archive* (New York: Redeemer Presbyterian Church, 2013).

29. Maclaren, *Expositions*, 254–55.

30. "The fact of their past progress and the assurance of the righteous judgment of the Lord are not sufficient to guarantee that the readers will stand firm in their faith and share in the future blessings. Christian perseverance is a matter of continuing prayer and continuing faith," (Marshall, *1 and 2 Thessalonians*, 181).

own effort. "Man needs the help of God as he seeks to work his will."[31] It is our Father who should receive credit for our goodness, not ourselves (cf. Matt 5:16). If we spend eternity in his awe-inspiring presence, it will be due to God's faithfulness. After all, "the very essence of heaven is the eradication of our selfishness, our transformation into Christ's image, and our preoccupation with his glory."[32]

There is disagreement on how to translate or interpret the phrase "make you worthy" (1:11; cf. "count you worthy," NASU). "Make you worthy" is often understood as God qualifying us until we actually deserve or are worthy of eternal reward. The other suggested translation, "to consider," implies that God thinks we are something we are not and could never be. Though the ESV reads "count you worthy" in 2 Thess 1:11, it translates the same Greek verb as "count" or "consider" elsewhere in the NT (e.g. Luke 7:7; 1 Tim 5:17). For these reasons, I believe Paul was praying for God to consider the Thessalonians worthy of his calling.[33] God works in us to accomplish our salvation, but saving us from eternal punishment is not the ultimate goal of his work. We are saved in order to bring glory to God's name (Pss 23:3; 25:11; 79:9; 106:8; 1 John 2:12). Here, Paul affirms that God's power was at work in the Thessalonians "so that the name of our Lord Jesus may be glorified in you, and you in him, according to the grace of our God and the Lord Jesus Christ" (2 Thess 1:12 NIV). Considering the Thessalonians were a persecuted people, the conversation is appropriately steered in the direction of Christ's glory, the perfect focal point for an oppressed people.

To surrender completely to God—to be his property—is to resign ourselves to suffering in this life. It is inevitable and unavoidable. A world that does not know or obey God will never understand our allegiance to the King. Afflicted on every side, Christians can still rest securely in the

---

31. Kelcy, Letters, 148. "Paul does not ascribe to God's grace merely the beginning of our salvation but every part of it," (Calvin, 1, 2 Thessalonians, 80).

32. Stott, Message of Thessalonians, 153.

33. cf. Beale, 1–2 Thessalonians, 194; BDAG 94.

knowledge that suffering makes us worthy of God's Kingdom, that Jesus will return and avenge injustice, and that we will be glorified in Christ forever and ever. May such a wonderful hope increase our faith and love!

TALKING POINTS

Paul's prayer for the Thessalonians is the same prayer he would offer up for us: that our faith grow abundantly and our love increase for one another. Calvin suggested all Christians take time each day to reflect on how they have grown in these areas.[34] In every season of life, faith is absolutely necessary to please God (Heb 11:6), because he uses both critical and seemingly unimportant moments to increase our faith. We may not like how he does it, but faith is never tested (and therefore strengthened) as when we are tempted or persecuted. In short, our faith only increases when we are forced to trust God on a deeper level than previously demanded. In the same way, our capacity to love is challenged daily in both large and small ways. We think of loving our enemies in terms of loving those who are different from us, whether it is racially, politically, or religiously. Such love is often impersonal; it doesn't demand we get our hands dirty. Paul was grateful that the Thessalonians' love for one another was increasing, particularly when none are more difficult to love sincerely than our physical and spiritual family members. Regardless of the circumstances, God desires our faith and love to increase until our King returns, for this is what brings him glory, praise, and thanksgiving.

It's a fundamental truth of life that, sometimes, the worst things happen to the best people. Whenever we are mistreated by others, we are tempted to blame God, to make him the object of our anger and disappointment. After all, if he were indeed an all-loving, all-powerful God, he would never allow such horrible things to happen, right? God is not responsible for the wickedness around us; he cannot tempt anyone with sin (Jas 1:13), and he has sworn "to repay with affliction those who afflict" us (2 Thess 1:6; cf. Rom 12:19). Regardless, there remain many times when we are disappointed with the Lord. The author of the 73rd Psalm expressed despair over the success and easy living of the wicked

---

34. Calvin, *1, 2 Thessalonians*, 74.

in comparison to the suffering of the righteous. The writer is perplexed about this, and it seems to almost undermine his faith, until he explains, "I went into the sanctuary of God; then I discerned their [the wicked's] end" (Ps 73:17). He recalls that the wicked, though they may prosper in this life, are nevertheless destined for God's wrath. The righteous, however, know "it is good to be near God" and seek refuge in him (73:28). Just as Scripture reveals how natural it is to be disappointed with God, it also encourages us to vent our frustration to him and seek comfort in his presence and his Word. Studying Scripture and seeking fellowship with Christ remind us that, for all the things the wicked might possess, deliverance from coming wrath is not, nor will ever be, one of them. As another psalmist puts it, "Better is one day in your courts than a thousand elsewhere" (Ps 84:10 NIV).

A t the risk of alienating you, I have a confession to make. While reading this passage, it was easy for me to descend into vindictive, sinister scorn for the wicked as Paul narrated what awaits them on the final day. Such is a product of my desire for vengeance and retribution for those who have wronged me. Desiring justice is not wrong; God is just, and Paul is adamant that God's prerogative to punish is just as well. The problem with my insatiable thirst for justice is that it is self-centered. I shamefully admit that my desire for vengeance concerns those who have wronged me personally, not so much those who were profoundly wicked (e.g. Hitler, Stalin, Hussein). I repent of that, since I have come to realize that "in the holy love of God there is no room for petty spite or malice."[35] As Christians, when we read this passage, we should pray for God to replace our vindictiveness with gratitude for his unparalleled justice and for the privilege to suffer for his glory in this life.

---

35. Ward, *Commentary*, 142.

8

KING OF SINFUL SOTS

In the 1970s, Hal Lindsey released his bestseller, *The Late Great Planet Earth*. His book launched a renewed firestorm of interest in the Second Coming within Christian circles. Along with that interest came a revival of the debate concerning the identity of the Antichrist, a person to whom Lindsey devoted an entire chapter, calling him "the Future Führer."

The designation *Antichrist* is a misnomer, particularly in any end-times conversation. Too often, we forget that the term never occurs in the book of Revelation, which is where you would expect it to pop-up with great frequency. Its use is restricted solely to 1–2 John. Paul, however, speaks of an end-times figure in 2 Thess 2, which bears a striking resemblance to the Antichrist concept in John's letters. The apostle calls this character the "man of lawlessness" and "son of perdition," a figure that will arise and wield tremendous power before the return of Christ. Of course, we are not told *how soon* this man will appear before the Second Coming—only that he will.

The passage on the man of lawlessness may be the primary reason Paul wrote this letter. At the very least, it is "the most distinctive feature of 2 Thessalonians,"[1] and outside the book of Revelation, I consider these verses to be the most difficult in the NT.[2] There is a great deal of

---

1. Bruce, *1 & 2 Thessalonians*, 162.

2. "Readers of the New Testament stumbling for the first time into the middle of 2

ambiguity in the passage, which has proven to be a catalyst for many wild interpretations. It is vague because Paul references prior instruction he had provided on the subject (2:5), teachings to which we were not privy. "It is precisely because Paul feels that he can assume so much on the part of his readers that the modern reader has so much difficulty in understanding the passage."[3]

We should therefore engage this passage with a significant dose of humility and confessed ignorance.[4] We cannot know exactly what Paul is discussing here, but we are told enough to prevent our hearts from being "quickly shaken" and "alarmed." Peter assured us that God has given us, not necessarily comprehensive knowledge on every subject, but rather what is necessary to live a godly life (2 Pet 1:3).

In his previous letter to the Thessalonians, Paul had written a considerable amount on the Second Coming. He assured his readers that those who had already died in Christ would not miss out on that great day (4:13–17), and that it would come very quickly, so the Thessalonians needed to be ever vigilant (5:1–10). After this first letter, however, it appears either a bogus letter from Paul or a new false teacher had come to Thessalonica, claiming that the day of the Lord had come and gone. The Thessalonians believed they had missed it! Was it because they had not heeded Paul's exhortation? "So let's not sleepwalk through life like those others. Let's keep our eyes open and be smart" (1 Thess 5:6 Msg). The apostle's response to their despair and panic reassured them: "No,

---

Thessalonians may be forgiven if they feel like Alice tumbling down a dark hole into Wonderland," (Gaventa, *Thessalonians*, 107). "This is an extraordinarily difficult passage, not made any easier by the fact that its subject matter is not dealt with elsewhere," (Morris, *Thessalonians*, 217).

3. Marshall, *1 and 2 Thessalonians*, 185.

4. "Church history is littered with incautious, self-confident but mistaken attempts to find in Paul's text a reference to some contemporary person and event. Let this be a warning to us to be more cautious and tentative than some others have been. At the same time, we have no liberty to abandon the task as hopeless, for 2 Thessalonians 2 is an important part of Scripture, which has been written and preserved for the church's instruction," (Stott, *Message of Thessalonians*, 161–62).

you have not missed the return of Christ. Some things must happen first before that great day comes."

When I first discovered this chapter, I admit to being flabbergasted. All my life, I had believed the Second Coming and the end of all things to be an event that would take place at any moment, but without obvious build-up or any warning whatsoever. I took seriously the NT imagery of this event coming like a thief in the night. Paul, however, is emphatic that there will be events—notable events—that precede Jesus' return. As I have already mentioned, Paul does not answer all of our questions, and at times, provokes new questions. He does, however, give us enough information to provide peace for our troubled hearts.

2 THESSALONIANS 2:1-2

The opening verse of 2 Thess 2 has Paul turning his focus to the Second Coming, an event he had previously narrated in 1 Thess 4:13-17. But now the Thessalonians had been "quickly shaken" and "alarmed" at the incorrect notion that "the day of the Lord has come," i.e. that the last day and Christ's return were about to occur any day now.[5] We aren't talking about a mild irritation or annoyance, but something very unsettling.

The verb translated "shaken" (*saleuō*) was used in classical Greek to describe earthquakes and stormy seas rocking ships.[6] It was also used as a metaphor "of being so perturbed as to lose one's normal composure and good sense."[7] Philosophers used it of "people who were unstable in their opinions."[8] In the NT, it is also used of a reed shaken by the wind (Matt 11:7) and a tree disturbed by a gale so that it loses its fruit (Rev 6:13; cf.

---

5. Shogren effectively argues that the Greek *enistēmi*, translated "has come," is better rendered "is near" (cf. "at hand," KJV) as in it is just about to happen (*1 & 2 Thessalonians*, 275–77). If the Thessalonians thought that Jesus had already come and gone, surely Paul would have told them such had not happened since "every eye will see him" at his coming (Rev 1:7).

6. NIDNTT 3:558.

7. Marshall, *1 and 2 Thessalonians*, 186.

8. Green, *Thessalonians*, 303.

Isa 7:2 LXX). When the early church prayed for boldness, God shook the house where they were praying to communicate his favor (Acts 4:31; cf. Heb 12:26); the wise man in Jesus' parable built a house that could not be shaken by a flash food (Luke 6:48; cf. Acts 16:26). It is not insignificant that David says he would not be "shaken" because the Lord and his instruction were always before him (Ps 16:7–8 LXX). The most ironic use of the word in the NT, however, is when the Thessalonian Jews came to Berea to "shake things up" against Paul and Silas (Acts 17:13).

Paul is also disappointed that they were "alarmed." Unlike "quickly shaken," "alarmed" is a present-tense verb, meaning this was an on-going condition for the Thessalonians. The shaking of their faith had resulted in an alarmed state,[9] i.e. they were suffering a "continuing state of mental disturbance"[10] with a "continued uneasiness and apprehension"[11] (cf. Matt 24:6). It's not unlike the panic we feel when a hurricane or tornado is heading in our direction. "The young believers had been shaken loose from their mental moorings and were adrift on a tossing sea of anxiety and fear, their faith, hope, and joy devastated by deception."[12]

The apostle blames the disturbance on any one of three things: a bogus prophecy,[13] preacher,[14] or letter.[15] I don't think Paul is referring to 1 Thessalonians when he mentions "a letter seeming to be from us." "If

---

9. "A continued state of agitation following upon a definite shock received," (George Milligan, *St. Paul's Epistles to the Thessalonians* [London: Macmillan, 1908], 96).

10. Wanamaker, *Thessalonians*, 239.

11. Ward, *Commentary*, 154.

12. John MacArthur, *1 & 2 Thessalonians* (Chicago: Moody Press, 2002), 269.

13. The Greek literally reads "a spirit," which is most often interpreted as a prophetic utterance (cf. 1 Thess 5:19–20; 1 John 4:1–3).

14. "We might caution modern Christians to understand that the message of every radio or television preacher, or even every person who stands behind a pulpit, needs to be examined through the lens of apostolic teaching as contained in Scripture," (Green, *Thessalonians*, 305).

15. "It was not only persecutors who were disturbing the peace of the Thessalonian church; it was false teachers as well. In fact, the intellectual assault on Christianity is often fiercer than the physical," (Stott, *Message of Thessalonians*, 156).

he believed that the misunderstanding came from his previous letter, he would have sought simply to make clearer what he had said before, not alluded to three possible sources of misunderstanding."[16] Paul concluded this current letter by calling attention to his "distinguishing mark" (2 Thess 3:17 NIV), as if he was conscious of the existence of a forged letter. Whatever the source, news that the Second Coming had already occurred had caused a lot of distress in Thessalonica. Paul is concerned because he knows such information was false, but had still deceived his brethren.

We are not privy to all the information known to the Thessalonians. Paul admits that he is only rehearsing the main points (2 Thess 2:5), but this leads me to ask: "Why are you so ambiguous, Paul?" It seems best to suggest that Paul was intentionally ambiguous in his writing so that, if the letter fell into the wrong hands, the Thessalonians would not be persecuted any more than they already were. We must remember that, in Thessalonica, the accusation had been made that Paul and his companions were proclaiming a rival to the Emperor's throne.

2 THESSALONIANS 2:3–8

In these verses, Paul relates a particular chain of events that will climax with the return of Christ. This passage was meant to comfort the Thessalonians and to remind them of what was to come.

Restraint. In 2 Thess 2:6–7, Paul says something is restraining or preventing the man of lawlessness from being revealed, but that at some point, the Restrainer will be removed.[17] The ambiguity is compounded by the fact that Paul refers to this Restrainer in the neuter gender in 2:6,

---

16. Witherington, *1 and 2 Thessalonians*, 214. Beale, however, disagrees: "The common wording and theme show that this section is a further unpacking of 1 Thessalonians 4:14–17 and that the false teaching is an overrealized distortion of that part of Paul's first letter," (*1–2 Thessalonians*, 200; cf. Malherbe, *Thessalonians*, 416).

17. Most interpreters assume the Restrainer to be a positive force, not negative, but there is not universal agreement on this (cf. Paul S. Dixon, "The Evil Restraint in 2 Thess 2:6," *JETS* 33 [1990]: 445–49).

but uses the masculine gender in 2:7. Simply put, is the Restrainer an impersonal force (e.g. the rule of law) or a living being (e.g. a political leader)? An it or a he? Is it possible that Paul means both? I think he does, describing perhaps a force embodied by a person.[18]

Early Christian writers (e.g. Tertullian, *Apology* 32.29) believed the Roman Empire was the restraining force, keeping the man of lawlessness at bay for a time. This opinion would certainly explain why Paul seems so guarded in his comments. If the Thessalonians were already in a bind because of their perceived unfaithfulness to Rome, then Paul's suggestion that the Empire was a restraining force could be interpreted as seditious and only fan the flames of persecution. Paul would later argue that civil government existed to restrain evil (Rom 13:1–5). "In the execution of this purpose the state is an instrument in the hands of God. When it violates that mandate, promoting evil and suppressing the good, it is demonic and the instrument of Satan."[19] Kaiser goes on to point out that Paul had recently been the beneficiary of Rome's (i.e. civil government's) restraining influence in Philippi (Acts 16:35–39) and in Corinth (Acts 18:12–17). Alfred Plummer says this view fits so well that "it is almost a waste of time to look for any other,"[20] especially since it explains the use of both neuter and masculine genders—"Think of the empire and the emperor, of justice and the judge, of law and the one who enforces it."[21]

A very similar interpretation is that the Restrainer is the force or principle of law and order. Morris prefers this interpretation, although he does not believe a choice is necessary.[22] It is hard to see how Paul considers the Restrainer to be Rome or civil government in general when

---

18. "In regard to the old debate about whether Paul is talking about a restraining force or a restraining person, the answer is simply Yes," (Witherington, *1 and 2 Thessalonians*, 221).

19. Kaiser, *Hard Sayings*, 663–64.

20. Alfred Plummer, *A Commentary on St. Paul's Second Epistle to the Thessalonians* (London: Scott, 1918), 60.

21. William Hendriksen, *Exposition of Thessalonians* (Grand Rapids: Baker, 1955), 182.

22. Morris, *Thessalonians*, 227.

he describes the Rebellion in purely religious terms. If Paul considered Rome to be the Restrainer in a positive way, why does he adopt such anti-imperial rhetoric in these two letters? Also, how exactly did the collapse of the Roman Empire signal the "beginning of the end"?

Another option is to interpret the Restraining power as the gospel, and the Restrainer as Paul himself. Once Paul is out of the way, the Rebellion and Revelation would come.[23] Green correctly points out that Paul nowhere else considered his preaching and ministry to be "holding the fort against the breakout of the personification of evil."[24] Plus, I have a difficult time seeing God purposely removing the preaching of the gospel at any point in time. It just doesn't explain why Paul was so guarded and cryptic in this present passage.

A similar suggestion is that the Restrainer is the Spirit working through the church. This would certainly make sense considering Jesus' comments about being salt and light (Matt 5:13–16). But one struggles to see how and when the church would ever be removed and the Spirit no longer active prior to Jesus' return.[25]

It would be nearly impossible for me to adequately exhaust the list of nominees for the Restrainer;[26] the reality is that every interpretation has its problems. So I have no choice but to concur with Augustine, who concluded in the end, "I frankly confess I do not know what he

---

23. Calvin, 1, 2 Thessalonians, 90–91.

24. Green, Thessalonians, 315. Witherington further observes, "He does not envision a time when the gospel will be removed from the scene. Indeed in parallel material in Mark 13 we are told that the gospel must be proclaimed throughout the many nations before the end can come," (1 and 2 Thessalonians, 210).

25. "There are no traditions in the NT about the Spirit ever being withdrawn again after Pentecost," (Witherington, 1 and 2 Thessalonians, 210).

26. "In the long and complex history of the interpretations of this passage, every possible alternative to the identification of this restraining force or person has been suggested. I'm sure that one would be safe in offering a cash reward to anyone who could offer an option not yet suggested," (Demarest, 1, 2 Thessalonians, 121).

means,"[27] (*City of God* 20.19.2). On the other hand, it is almost certain the Thessalonians understood Paul, because after reminding them of the teaching he had delivered in person (2:5), he says, "You know what is restraining him" (2:6).

Rebellion. There are two more events that must take place simultaneously, instead of consecutively.[28] One is a large-scale apostasy (the word Paul actually uses is the Greek *apostasia*), something called "the Rebellion." In secular contexts, the word was used of political or military revolts (Josephus, *Antiquities* 13.219). In the LXX (e.g. Josh 22:22; 2 Chr 28:19; 33:19; Jer 2:19) and the NT (Matt 24:12; Acts 21:21; 1 Tim 4:1–3; 2 Tim 3:1–9), it naturally meant a rebellion against God. Even in Jewish literature, a rebellion against God was expected before the end of all things.[29] The term *apostasia* inherently requires a departure away and against something previously followed, and in this case, "a deliberate defection from a formerly held religious position."[30] It's impossible to rebel against God if you have never followed him or submitted to his rule, which implies that the Rebellion will be of the faithful, not the heathen.[31]

But it is not definite that Paul means a rebellion against God; he simply calls it "the Rebellion." Some scholars believe Paul is referring to a "a general abandonment of the basis of civil order."[32] I find this option

---

27. "Attempts to identify this restrainer are not quite so multitudinous as attempts to identify the lawless one, but they are just as futile," (Gaventa, *Thessalonians*, 113). "The plain fact is that Paul and his readers knew what he was talking about, and we do not. We have not the means at our disposal to recover this part of his meaning. It is best that we frankly acknowledge our ignorance," (Morris, *Thessalonians*, 228).

28. "The *prōton* ('first') is to be taken with both the apostasy and the revelation of the Man of Lawlessness," (Malherbe, *Thessalonians*, 418).

29. 1 Enoch 93:9; 90:26; 2 Esdras 5:1–13; 2 Baruch 41:3; 42:4; Jubilees 23:14–21.

30. MacArthur, *1 & 2 Thessalonians*, 272.

31. "Now, nobody can be called an apostate but he who had previously professed to follow Christ and the Gospel. Paul, therefore, is predicting a general rebellion in the visible church," (Calvin, *1, 2 Thessalonians*, 87).

32. Bruce, *1 & 2 Thessalonians*, 167.

difficult to accept since *apostasia* almost always carries a religious nuance in the NT. Others believe this is a rebellion against God, specifically on the part of the Jews. A similar interpretation, one I believe to be very plausible, is that this is a reference to the Jewish rebellion against Rome that began in A.D. 67 and culminated in the destruction of Jerusalem. In this instance, Paul would be warning that the Jewish nation would rebel and be punished severely (cf. 1 Thess 2:14–16). Since this had not yet happened, Jesus could not have returned yet. There are also those who interpret this Rebellion as large-scale apostasy by the church.[33] Considering Jesus' comments in Matt 24, Mark 13, I believe this last option to be as equally plausible as the second. One thing that is *not* uncertain, as we will see in 2 Thess 2:13–15, is that Paul hoped the Thessalonians "would in no way participate in the apostasy."[34]

Revelation. Along with the Rebellion, Paul says the man of lawlessness will be simultaneously revealed, a figure he also describes as the son of perdition. More than lawless, this man actually exists in opposition to law, particularly God's Law. This is his character. That he is a "son of destruction" describes his destiny.[35] The only other person to earn this terrible moniker is Judas Iscariot (John 17:12). As damnable as Judas' betrayal was, the sin of the man of lawlessness will be worse.[36] He is so opposed to God that he usurps God's central place in the temple[37] and

---

33. Beale, *1–2 Thessalonians*, 203–4; Green, *Thessalonians*, 307. "The pressure under which the faithful will find themselves will cause many of their number to defect," (Malherbe, *Thessalonians*, 418).

34. Green, *Thessalonians*, 307.

35. "In the NT the term commonly has to do with the destruction of those who oppose God and his purposes (Matt. 7.13; Rom. 9.22; Phil. 1.28; 3.19; Heb. 10.39; 2 Pet. 3.7; Rev. 17.8, 11)," (Ibid., 308–9).

36. "He is fixed for punishment and judgment; he is human trash for the garbage dump of hell," (MacArthur, *1 & 2 Thessalonians*, 273).

37. Speculation as to what Paul meant by "temple" here is yet another thorn in this very ambiguous passage. Is he referring to the Jerusalem Temple destroyed in A.D. 70? A future Temple yet to be built on the same site? Is it a metaphor for heaven or the church? Each of these options poses as many problems as they have supporters. Personally, I consider Paul's reference

claims to be God himself (cf. Isa 14:4–20; Ezek 28:1–10; Dan 11:36). The Bible knows no greater act of rebellion than to seize positions of authority and honor belonging to God alone.

The question is inevitable, so we should ask it now: Who is the man of lawlessness? Is he identifiable with any past historical figure? If he is to come in the future, how will we recognize him? Past suggestions have included Satan, Judaism, Caesar (usually Nero, but also Titus and Domitian),[38] several dictators (e.g. Napoleon, Hitler) and U.S. Presidents,[39] Barney the Dinosaur (my vote), computers, the Internet, and the fictional Nicolae Jetty Carpathia of the *Left Behind* series.[40] People have put forth these nominations with disturbing levels of gravity.

More viable candidates have included the pope (pick a pope, any pope) and, by extension, the Catholic Church. In fact, Catholicism and/ or the papacy are the most common identification among Protestant commentators.[41] The Westminster Confession calls the pope "that man of sin, and son of perdition, that exalteth himself, in the Church, against Christ and all that is called God." Spurgeon was so sure of this identification that he quipped, "If this 'man of sin' be not the Pope of Rome, we cannot tell who is

---

to the temple here to be a figure of speech, highlighting how the man of lawlessness will stop at nothing in his quest to usurp God (cf. Marshall, *1 and 2 Thessalonians*, 192). For a better survey of all the interpretive options, see Shogren, *1 & 2 Thessalonians*, 282–84.

38. "The divine claim of the emperor celebrated in the imperial cult was thus the prototype of the 'man of lawlessness,' and the Thessalonian believers would have understood this allusion well," (Green, *Thessalonians*, 310).

39. Since Gerald Burton Winrod, "almost every president has landed on the Antichrist suspect list. FDR, JFK, Nixon, Ronald Reagan, Bill Clinton, and Barack Obama have all been named by various individuals and organizations. The one exception to the rule may be Gerald Ford. Despite being a world leader during the height of the 1970s End Times craze, it's unlikely anyone ever considered Ford a serious contender for the title of Antichrist," (Joe Carter, "The 7 Most Popular Contenders for the Title 'Antichrist,'" The Gospel Coalition, http://thegospelcoalition.org/blogs/tgc/2012/11/16/the-7-most-popular-contenders-for-the-antichrist, accessed October 28, 2013).

40. Holmes gives a much more comprehensive list (*1 and 2 Thessalonians*, 241).

41. Wayne Jackson, *Revelation* (Stockton, CA: Christian Courier, 2004), 128–30.

the antichrist,"[42] (cf. the Preface to the KJV). Calvin was equally confident: "Everyone who has learned from Scripture what things especially belong to God will have no great difficulty in recognizing the Antichrist as he observes the claims of the Pope, even if he is only a ten-year-old boy."[43] Catholicism, however, hardly opposes "every so-called god or object of worship" (2 Thess 2:4), and it has existed for well over a millennium, though Paul seems to intimate that the man of lawlessness will be revealed just before Jesus' return (how soon, we cannot know). Moreover, he seems to have an individual in mind, rather than "a line of ecclesiastics."[44]

Here is what we are told specifically about this man from the text. After the Rebellion begins, there will come the revelation of this man of lawlessness. This person is against, and considers himself superior to, every other object of worship—even God himself (cf. Dan 11:36–37). He had not yet appeared when 2 Thessalonians was written by Paul, though "the mystery of lawlessness [was] already at work" (2 Thess 2:7). This man will be empowered by Satan and deceive many with false miracles, but Jesus will nevertheless destroy him effortlessly on the last day.

There were certainly historical figures before Paul's time who could have qualified for this man of lawlessness.[45] I want to stress, however, that these people had already come and gone, whereas Paul clearly indicated the man to be a future figure. Consider:

• Two centuries earlier, Antiochus IV Epiphanes had dared to raise himself up against God and the Temple, and while

42. C. H. Spurgeon, *The Metropolitan Tabernacle Pulpit Sermons*, vol. 52 (London: Passmore, 1906), 312.

43. Calvin, *1, 2 Thessalonians*, 89.

44. Morris, *Thessalonians*, 221. He comments further, "This view seems to have arisen more from hostility to the papacy than from exegetical considerations."

45. Given these three "forerunners" of the man of lawlessness, Stott concludes that this figure "may during the course of church history have had (and still have) multiple fulfilments, and that we would be unwise to look for only one in such a way as to pronounce all the others false," (*Message of Thessalonians*, 165).

he was successful for a time, God eventually dropped the hammer on his tyrannical rule (cf. Dan 8, 11).

- In 63 B.C., the Roman general Pompey conquered Jerusalem and desecrated the Most Holy Place by entering it. In the non-inspired Psalms of Solomon 17:11–22 (c. 48 B.C.), the author refers to Pompey as "the lawless one."

- About ten years prior to the composition of 2 Thessalonians, the Roman Emperor Caligula tried unsuccessfully to install a statue of himself in the Temple in Jerusalem. The Jewish backlash against this plan was so intense that Rome's local officials stalled for time, and Caligula was assassinated before he could press the issue further (Josephus, *Antiquities* 18.261–309).

I have no real desire to attempt identification of the man of lawlessness because I simply cannot do so. It's as simple as that. Gaventa says it best: "The quest to learn the name of this figure has proved irresistible to Christians across the centuries. Perhaps we sense that, if we have the [man of lawlessness'] name, we will have power over that figure as Jesus demanded the names of the evil spirits he ousted."[46]

I would love to be the person who correctly identified this king of sinful sots, but everyone else has struck out attempting to do so, and something tells me I would fare no better. In addition, if God intended us to easily identify this man, he would have left us more clues. The endless speculation might just constitute trespassing on territory that belongs exclusively to the Father—and this is exactly what the man of lawlessness will do (2:4)![47] Finally, there is danger in getting bogged down in the details of a difficult passage at the expense of the main point.[48] Paul was uninterested in explicitly

---

46. Gaventa, *Thessalonians*, 113.

47. Jacob W. Elias, *1 and 2 Thessalonians* (Scottdale, PA: Herald Press, 1995), 295.

48. "It is deeply ironic that some people get so caught up in speculation that they end up giving more attention to a doomed Antichrist than they do to the victorious Christ," (Holmes, *1 and 2 Thessalonians*, 241). His words echo the question Arno Gaebelein asked in 1933: "Why

naming the man of lawlessness or the Restrainer because he had a greater purpose in mind: reminding the Thessalonians of the truth.

Retribution. Since he had already described this event in 2 Thess 1, Paul does not spend more time on the subject. He only adds that Christ will bring retribution and punishment upon the man of lawlessness (as well as all evil) when he returns (2 Thess 2:8). Specifically, Jesus will destroy him "with the breath of his mouth," an event prophesied as early as Isaiah: "One breath from his mouth will destroy the wicked" (Isa 11:4 NLT). At his coming, astride his warhorse with sword in hand, Jesus "will release the fierce wrath of God, the Almighty, like juice flowing from a winepress" (Rev 19:15 NLT; cf. 1 Cor 15:24). There will be no dramatic showdown at Armageddon. No epic struggle. The Lord Jesus need only appear and breathe, and then the greatest human embodiment of evil will be tossed aside like a ratty chew toy. Satan's greatest warrior will be to the holy wrath of God what a dandelion is to a hurricane.

We are not told how much time will transpire on earth between the revelation of the man of lawlessness and the return of Christ. His reign of terror could number in days or millennia. Scripture is uninterested in spelling out the *when* of the Second Coming. Instead, it tells us what we can be certain of, namely, that Jesus will return as the conquering King to be glorified, he will vindicate his saints, and will destroy all his enemies once and for all.

What a day, glorious day, that will be.

2 THESSALONIANS 2:9-12

Only after Paul has assured his readers of the man of lawlessness' ultimate doom does he further narrate his activity. Just as Jesus will have a "coming," so too will this man. Such an event will be by Satan's active power (cf. Rev 13:2) and will be accompanied "with all power and false signs and

---

should a Christian have any interest at all in that coming man of sin? We have nothing to do with that lawless one. Our interest must be in Christ and not in Antichrist," ("King Feisal Is Dead," *Our Hope* 40 [Nov 1933]: 305).

wonders," just as Jesus predicted (Mark 13:22). Paul is not speaking of false miracles in the sense that they aren't real; they are false because they are not from God and thus do not lead to the truth. This lawless agent of Satan will have authentic powers, but they will be deceptive.

These signs will deceive, but only those who have already chosen to reject the truth of the gospel.[49] As far back as the pharaoh of the Exodus, God has allowed hearts to be hardened and deceived in order to accomplish his will and glorify himself.[50] God has even allowed Satan to work in order to achieve the divine purpose (cf. 2 Sam 24:1; 1 Chr 21:1; 1 Kgs 22:23).

It cannot be overstated that God is not an active player in the deception, for he cannot lie[51] (Tit 1:2; Heb 6:18). He only *allows* the delusion to come upon those who have already rejected him (cf. Eph 4:17–19). As one of my college professors put it, "The lost become more lost." Paul spoke elsewhere of how "the god of this world has blinded the minds of the unbelievers, to keep them from seeing the light of the gospel of the glory of Christ" (2 Cor 4:4; cf. 2 Cor 11:3; 1 Tim 2:14). God hands us over to deception and destruction by allowing us to have free will, and thus experience the full force of the consequences of our actions (Rom 1:24–28; 11:8; 2 Tim 4:4). "Through sin, sin is punished."[52] Perhaps this final point is best illustrated by the famous passage in C. S. Lewis' *The Great Divorce*. "There are only two kinds of people in the end: those who say to God, 'Thy will be done,' and those to whom God says, in the end, '*Thy* will be done.' All that are in Hell, choose it. Without that self-choice there could be no Hell."[53]

---

49. "It is not just any lie that these people will accept, but Satan's last and greatest piece of deception, the lie that the Man of Lawlessness is God," (Morris, *Thessalonians*, 234).

50. Exod 4:21; 7:3, 13, 22; 8:15, 32; 9:12, 34; 10:1, 20, 27; 11:10; 13:15; 14:4, 8, 17; cf. Isa 19:14; 29:9–10; Ezek 14:9.

51. "God does not deceive. Deception is the work of the lawless one (v. 10). What he sends is error-and-its-moral-consequences, its outworking: a cancer, not a bullet," (Ward, *Commentary*, 162).

52. Ibid.

53. C. S. Lewis, *The Great Divorce* (New York: HarperCollins, 2000), 75.

C onsidering the disheartening level of ambiguity in this passage, it is hard to believe that there are any firm conclusions to be drawn that can edify God's people. However, I believe there are three.[54]

First, there is evil in the world, and the level of evil will only increase as we draw nearer to the last day. It seems the Rebellion of which Paul spoke still lies in the future. Therefore, any feeling we have that the world is improving may be attributed to Satan's lie, rather than gospel truth.

Second, God is in complete control. "History is not a random series of meaningless events. It is rather a succession of periods and happenings which are under the sovereign rule of God, who is the God of history."[55] In this passage, Paul speaks of the "mystery" (i.e. something now concealed) of lawlessness, and that the man of lawlessness will be "revealed in his time." Who is it that has commanded this man to be concealed and later revealed "in his time"? The same One who makes known the end from the beginning (Isa 46:10)![56] Who is sovereign over this man but the Creator, Sustainer, and Lord of all things? Friend, if you neglect this point, then you neglect one of the very reasons Paul wrote these two letters. There is no comfort to be gained from this passage unless we first confess that God is in control. He is sovereign, even over unimaginable wickedness. Jesus will demonstrate his supremacy at his coming when he is glorified as the returning, conquering King.

Finally, the only unknown factor in this passage that is worthy of our concern is this: What will be *our* response to the truth of Christ's gospel? Will we be among those who are deceived by Satan because we hated the truth? Or will we love and believe the truth,[57] thereby opening our hearts

---

54. Barclay, *Letters*, 213.

55. Stott, *Message of Thessalonians*, 173.

56. "No wicked person, be he Satan, be he the Man of Lawlessness, be he anyone else whatever, can overstep the bounds God has appointed him. The Man of Lawlessness will be revealed only as and when God permits," (Morris, *Thessalonians*, 228).

57. "Not merely must we assent to, but *love*, the truth," (Robert Jamieson, A. R. Fausset, and David Brown, *A Commentary Critical, Experimental and Practical on the Old and New Testament*,

to the sanctifying work of the Spirit? Will we eschew the self-centered, deluded lies of the evil one? Or will we delight in unrighteousness, rejecting instead the selfless sacrifices of our Savior? If we have accepted Jesus and his gospel with open arms, we have no reason to fear anything that lies in the past, present, or future. Not even the man of lawlessness.

vol. 6 [Grand Rapids: Eerdmans, 1948], 476).

TALKING POINTS

The unnamed author of Hebrews encouraged another group of Christians facing severe persecution and affliction: "Let us not neglect our meeting together, as some people do, but encourage one another, especially now that the day of his return is drawing near" (Heb 10:25 NLT). Paul describes Jesus' return in 2 Thess 2:1 as a time when the church will be "gathered together" with Christ. Our assembly every week prepares us for the great assembly that will take place on the day of the Lord! As Ward puts it, one is a miniature and preparation for the other, and if we willingly infrequent the assembly every Lord's Day, we will certainly miss the great assembly on the Day of the Lord.[58] It is in the weekly assembly on the Lord's Day that we share communion and "proclaim the Lord's death until he comes" (1 Cor 11:26). It is in the assembly that we search the Scriptures so that Satan might not deceive us. It is in the assembly that our hope in Christ's return is renewed. With so many deceivers in the world, we need regular reminders of what is true. To paraphrase the author of Hebrews, don't forsake the assembly on the Lord's Day, or you will miss the great assembly on the day of the Lord!

When many of us think about the grand cosmic battle between good and evil, God and Satan, we know theoretically that God wins in the end. I can't help but feel, however, as if we imagine this scenario in terms of two sports teams battling it out: the momentum swings in one direction, then another, back and forth until the winner finally pulls it out with a dramatic grand slam or long-range field goal. Listen, church! Such a notion is as blasphemous as it is false! "This is not a contest between God and Satan in which God turns out to be a little stronger than Satan. God is sovereign over all, and uses even evil (in Satan and in people) to set forward his purpose."[59] Satan's greatest agent of sin and evil *will be blown*

---

58. Ward, *Commentary*, 153.

59. Leon Morris, *The Epistles of Paul to the Thessalonians*, Rev. ed. (Grand Rapids:

away by the full force of Jesus' glory! Jesus need only breathe on this man of lawlessness to destroy him completely. We are not told about this evil so that we might fear it, but that we might rest secure in the knowledge that God will glorify himself by delivering us from every threat to our souls. Hallelujah! Praise God! May the overwhelming nature of Christ's glorious presence comfort you whenever you fear the evil days that lie ahead. Or, as Jesus put it, "Take heart; I have overcome the world" (John 16:33).

Eerdmans, 1984), 135.

9

THE LOOKING GLASS

Since I was a very little boy, I've been fascinated with mirrors. It's not that I'm overly vain or that I enjoy looking at myself. Rather, I am fascinated with how mirrors are made. According to reliable sources (OK, so I just looked it up on Wikipedia), mirrors are nothing but a piece of glass coated on one side with either silver or aluminum. This is what gives the mirror its reflective characteristic. Remove the metal application, and all you're left with is clear glass—nothing but windowpane.

This next-to-last section of 2 Thessalonians reminds me of windows and mirrors. So far in this letter, Paul has explained the terrible fate of the wicked to be realized when our Lord returns (1:8–9). Whenever God's people suffer, we are comforted and reassured in knowing that evil people will get what's coming to them. Paul also discussed how the wicked have been deceived and deluded because they did not love the truth (2:10–11). Christians should rejoice, as the apostle does in 2:13, that we are among the saved, rather than the lost.

But why? To what or whom do we owe this marvelous condition? The answer comes down to whether you view the lost through a window or a mirror. It's easy to look down on the wicked with arrogance: "If only you were as moral or spiritual as me, maybe you wouldn't be a dirty rotten sinner in the hands of an angry God." Satan is the master of planting the seeds of elitism in the hearts of God's people, and those seeds bring forth the hideous fruit of pride and exclusivism. As Jonathan Swift, the 17th century Irish poet satirized, "We are God's chosen few / All others will be damned / There is no room in heaven for you / We can't have heaven crammed." We might think we're saved because we behave or believe better than others, because we are in the right church, or because our theological understanding is more mature than everyone else. In short, we think we are saved because we're better than the lost.

Nothing could be further from the truth.

In commenting on this passage, Calvin said, "We must think about the judgments of God on the reprobate in such a way that they are, as it were, mirrors that show us his mercy toward us. We must conclude that it is solely due to the special grace of God that we do not perish along with them."[1] If we contemplate the lost as through a window, we risk breeding arrogance. But if we see them as in a mirror, we are reminded that we would receive their fate were it not for the amazing grace of God. I confess to you that I have read 2 Thess 1–2 in the past and rubbed my hands in sadistic glee at the thought of the destiny of God's enemies. I have since repented of that, for God takes no pleasure in the demise of the wicked (Ezek 18:23; 2 Pet 3:9), but rather desires all to be saved (1 Tim 2:4), and he would surely not condone such an attitude.

There is some difficulty in teaching the material found in 2 Thess 2:13–3:5. As Holmes points out, "There is little new here, as Paul is for the most part reaffirming or reemphasizing points he has already made, whether in person or in the first letter."[2] Such reaffirmation isn't a bad thing. Paul is giving us the opportunity to rejoice and give thanks that we are among those destined for glory—not destruction—and only through the grace of God. This passage offers a contrast of what awaits those who are deceived by Satan versus those who love and obey the truth of Christ. We are also reminded through Paul's example of the importance of praying for

---

1. Calvin, *1, 2 Thessalonians*, 96.

2. Holmes, *1 and 2 Thessalonians*, 259.

one another in our spiritual struggle. The apostle both prays for, and solicits prayer from, his readers. May this passage be a mirror, a looking glass, in which you see a beautiful reflection of God's mercy and love for you.

2 THESSALONIANS 2:13-17

If 2 Thess 2:1–12 is the darkest portion of these two letters, the next three verses hearken the sunrise. In fact, I get the impression that Paul found no joy whatsoever in discussing the man of lawlessness. The subject was a necessary evil, and he used it only to accentuate the majesty of God. In direct contrast to the man of lawlessness, Paul says, is God's gracious election of the Thessalonians.

My decision to treat these verses in a separate chapter from the one on the man of lawlessness came with significant reservation. We must not divorce Paul's prayer in this section from the preceding conversation.[3] When God's people are challenged by evil and rebellion, they should do as Paul does: express thanksgiving for God's salvation. In 2:13–15, Paul gives thanks and instruction for the method, goal, and obligation of salvation.

Method. All salvation begins and ends with God. Salvation is his work.[4] We have no more right to boast of our salvation than a scalpel has in bragging about what a wonderful surgery it performed. God's election of the Thessalonian saints was verified or validated through two things: "sanctification by the Spirit and belief in the truth" (2:13). External

---

3. Fee points to several intriguing parallels between this section and 2:1–12 (e.g. sanctification vs. wickedness, the work of the Spirit vs. Satan, believing the truth vs. delighting in wickedness). Thus, the Thessalonians "stand in bold contrast to those who have not believed the truth and are thus destined to perish," (*Thessalonians*, 303). The language of this passage "is pastoral and has a comforting effect. Believers, who are aware of the mystery of lawlessness already at work and who know of the wickedness and deception still to come, may be comforted as they are reminded that they have been chosen by God and are at the center of his saving purpose," (Malherbe, *Thessalonians*, 438).

4. "Whereas in 1:3 he gave thanks for their demonstration of Christian virtues, here the stress lies more on what God is doing in their lives, and it is on this fact that he would build their assurance," (Marshall, *1 and 2 Thessalonians*, 206).

obedience to the plan of salvation has no effect unless we first subject ourselves to the Spirit's sanctifying work, thereby beginning the process of our being made holy, of becoming like Jesus. The fruit or proof of the Spirit's work in us is seen in how we practice love, joy, peace, etc. (Gal 5:22–23). Sanctification is not our work, but God's. Nonetheless, it is a process we must submit to; it does not come upon us against our will. It's not unlike hiring contractors to renovate your house: no honest person would take credit for their magnificent craftsmanship, but neither would the project have been done unless you solicited and consented to their work. It is the same with the Spirit's sanctifying work in our lives.

This submission or consent to the Spirit's work is what I think Paul had in mind when he spoke of the Thessalonians' "belief in the truth." Recall that in the previous section, Paul had spoken of those deceived by wickedness because they "refused to love the truth and so be saved" (2:10). To be sanctified—to become like Jesus—requires that we believe the truth. We must acknowledge our utter sinfulness before a holy God and invite him to purify our hearts through the cleansing work of Christ on the cross. Submission to the lordship of Jesus is a confession that all is not as it should be in our lives. The alternative is to pretend all is well in the midst of our sin, but only a deceived person continues in that delusion.

Goal. What is the purpose of our salvation? To what end or goal does God call us through the gospel? Paul says here that it is obtaining "the glory of our Lord Jesus Christ." The reason we live and long for the Lord in this life is so that we might be glorified with him in the next (Rom 8:17–18; Col 1:27). On the night before his death, Jesus prayed to the Father, "Glorify me in your own presence with the glory that I had with you before the world existed" (John 17:5).

Imagine the wonder, the amazement, the excitement of sharing and participating in such weighty glory, and for eternity! The same glory that God said he would never share with another (Isa 42:8; 48:11), he now extends to us through Christ! What an amazing thought, and how it must have caused the Thessalonians' hearts to soar when they heard these words! Can there be a greater cure for a heart burdened by "suffering for the Name" than to know we will one day be glorified along with our Savior and King?

Obligation. The doctrines of God's sovereignty and human responsibility are not as mutually exclusive as Calvinists and Arminians pretend. Paul has just finished describing God as both the agent and the end of salvation. The apostle then calls his readers to their subsequent obligation—"Stand firm and hold to the traditions." These commands are unnecessary if it is impossible to fall from grace (cf. Gal 5:4; Heb 12:15), but such is possible. The call to "stand firm"[5] and "hold to" represents our subsequent obligation in light of our salvation (cf. Rom 14:4; 1 Cor 16:13; Gal 5:1; Phil 1:27; 4:1).

When I think of Paul's command to "hold to," I recall the story of Henry Dempsey. In 1987, he was piloting a Beechcraft 99 for Eastern Express when he was sucked out of the plane mid-flight. He managed to survive by holding on to the rear stairs for ten minutes while his co-pilot landed at the airport in Portland, Maine. Imagine the death-grip Mr. Dempsey must have maintained on those stairs while the plane was at 4,000 feet and traveling at 190 miles per hour! He held on with every fiber of his being; it was either that or his death. We must hold to the traditions of Christ and the apostles with the same desperation.

Words evolve over time, taking on new meanings and nuance. In 1611, the KJV translators deemed "charity" to be the best expression of the love described in 1 Cor 13. Today, the word has evolved into a pejorative, an expression of condescending generosity (e.g. "I don't want your charity"). The term *literal* has also undergone a disturbing transition. In August 2013, the *London Telegraph* reported that the Oxford English Dictionary had added a new definition to the word in order to reflect its modern usage. To its standard (and correct) meaning, "in a literal way or sense," was added, "used for emphasis rather than being actually true."

---

5. Though they had been shaken and alarmed in 2:2, Paul now calls his readers to stand firm (McGarvey, *Thessalonians*, 43).

The paper went on to report that *literal* has been used, um, non-literally since Mark Twain penned *The Adventures of Tom Sawyer*, if not earlier.[6]

The literal evolution of *literal* is but a very small example of how the world is rapidly changing around us. The church has not been immune to this change. More to the point, tradition has become a bit of a dirty word in Christian circles. Even I am on record as saying, "'That's the way we've always done things' can be a self-righteous cop-out for cowards."[7] It is certainly true that some churches are stuck in a rut because they refuse to give up their traditions. There are certain traditions, however, that we must hold to, regardless of threat or circumstances, and they are the traditions that have been handed down to us from the apostles. Tradition receives a bad rap in certain places in the NT (e.g. Matt 15:3, 6; Gal 1:14; Col 2:8), but here, Paul means those truths he taught as a representative of Christ.[8] When he and the other apostles spoke, they did so with the authority of the risen Lord[9] (Matt 16:19 NASU), and as Stott put it, "Loyalty to apostolic teaching, now permanently enshrined in the New Testament, is still the test of truth and the shield against error."[10]

Paul further defined "traditions" as those things taught to the Thessalonians "either by our spoken word or by our letter" (2:15). Such

---

6. Steve Hawkes, "Uproar as OED includes erroneous use of 'literally'" *London Telegraph*, August 13, 2013.

7. Michael Whitworth, *The Epic of God* (Bowie, TX: Start2Finish Books, 2012), 259.

8. "It is no contradiction that Jesus repudiates tradition and Paul champions it. Paul's tradition agrees with Jesus' rejection, since they are both opposed to human tradition," (TDNT 2:172).

9. "We have no certain evidence of any thing having been delivered by [the apostles] more than what we find contained in the holy scriptures," (Henry, *Commentary*, 800).

10. Stott, *Message of Thessalonians*, 158. He wisely warns against interpreting in isolation vs. community. "Left to ourselves, it is easy for us to misinterpret the Word of God, to put on it constructions it was never intended to bear, and even to manipulate it to suit our prejudices. So we need the checks and balances of the Christian family, in order to help restrain our rampant individualism and establish us in the truth. It is the Bible in the church which can develop our Christian stability, and so strengthen us to withstand the pressures of persecution, false teaching and temptation," (179).

traditions act as guardrails on the narrow road winding its way up the mountain of holiness. Earlier, Paul pointed to false prophecy, teaching, or letter as culpable in the Thessalonians' hysteria concerning the day of the Lord (2:2). "'Pay attention,' Paul says, to what he and his companions actually taught them, not what someone is claiming or alleging they taught"[11]—lest unnecessary panic disturb the church once again.

Having reminded them of the threat of lawlessness, as well as the work of God, Paul concluded the section with a prayer. Once again, we are richly blessed to be able to hear the apostle's heavenly petition. In the face of all dangers, toils, and snares, Paul expressed the hope that God[12] would comfort and establish the Thessalonians. The obligation to stand firm and hold fast is ours, but salvation always remains the Lord's work. The reference to the God "who loved us" may refer to what happened at the cross, which is the ultimate proof of his divine love for us (Rom 5:8). The apostle goes further to say that the comfort and hope we receive from God are "through grace," meaning they are his unmerited gift to us.

There is a semi-significant variation in 2 Thess 2:13. The KJV, HCSB, NASU, and NKJV all read that God chose the Thessalonians "from the beginning." The ESV, NIV, NLT, and NRSV, however, have "as the firstfruits." Which is correct? Bruce Metzger explains the preference for "first fruits" over "from the beginning" by arguing that:

1. The Greek phrase *ap' arxēs* ("from the beginning") does not appear elsewhere in Paul's letters.

2. The Greek term translated "beginning" is almost always used by Paul to mean "power."

---

11. Holmes, *1 and 2 Thessalonians*, 253.

12. Many scholars comment on the high Christology evident in this passage. English readers will miss it, but Paul unmistakably equates the "Lord Jesus Christ" with "God our Father" in the Greek: the verbs "loved" and "gave" are singular, not plural.

3. The Greek term translated "firstfruits" occurs six other times in Paul's letters (Rom 8:23; 11:16; 16:5; 1 Cor 15:20, 23; 16:15).

4. We know that the medieval scribes altered "firstfruits" to "from the beginning" in Rom 16:5; Rev 14:4. It is possible that they did the same here.[13]

On the other hand, Leon Morris expresses his preference for "from the beginning" over "first fruits" by noting:

1. It's more likely that the scribes substituted "firstfruits" (a common Pauline expression) for "from the beginning," instead of vice versa.

2. Nowhere else in his letters does Paul use "firstfruits" in connection with God's election.

3. Morris notes that there is no qualifying genitive with "firstfruits" as is usual (e.g. "firstfruits of the Spirit," Rom 8:23).[14]

I am convinced that Paul wrote "from the beginning" instead of "firstfruits." Why does it matter? Considering that the apostle had just spoken of the man of lawlessness, a rebellion, and of the wicked being deceived, I'd say it matters a great deal. Paul rejoiced that the Thessalonians were a part of the church of Christ, that precious body of believers chosen "from the beginning for salvation" (2:13 NASU). Their salvation, therefore, was not in jeopardy because God always finishes what he starts (Phil 1:6). No threat against the church will ever stand, for she has been promised salvation from start to finish. We need not fear an oppressive government, a hostile culture, divisive infighting, or an unfaithful new generation. God has chosen us, the church, for salvation. This choice was made "from the

---

13. Metzger, *Textual Commentary*, 568.

14. Morris, *Thessalonians*, 239, n. 69.

beginning," which means God cast his eye over all history, assessed all threats, and still made his decision to redeem us. Let Satan, the man of lawlessness, and all the dark forces do their worst—they have no chance of hijacking the will of God. Let us, therefore, stand firm!

2 THESSALONIANS 3:1–5

The first five verses of 2 Thess 3 continue Paul's prayer, but with the addition that he now asks his readers to "pray for us,"[15] particularly for his ministry and safety. He prays again for his readers, but in a way that provides an amenable segue into the difficult issue of 3:6–15. First, he requests prayers for the gospel (cf. 2 Cor 1:11; Eph 6:19–20; Col 4:3–4), specifically that it would experience "free and rapid progress"[16] and receive the same reception in Corinth and beyond that it had in Thessalonica. Paul borrowed language from Ps 147:15—"He sends out his command to the earth; his word runs swiftly"—to express this desire. He employs the image of a runner because, just as athletes compete in order to win the prize, the apostle wished to see the gospel message outdistance its opponents and thereby be "honored"[17] (cf. "glorified," NASU). The gospel is glorified when it is obeyed (Acts 13:48), so Paul wished to see many respond to God's gracious offer of salvation.[18]

---

15. "He puts his imperative 'pray' in an emphatic position, which leaves no doubt as to the importance he attaches to it, and he puts it in the present continuous tense, so that it means 'pray continually,'" (Morris, *Thessalonians*, 245).

16. W. E. Vine and C. F. Hogg, *Expository Commentary on 1 & 2 Thessalonians* (Nashville: Nelson, 1997), 204. "And Paul longed that this word might 'run', that is, that it might make its way freely into people's hearts and lives, changing them and forming them into a holy and loving people who would bring God glory in the world. But often he must have felt as though, when he preached, the word of the Lord was like a runner in a dream: trying to do its work, but being held back by strange invisible forces, hardly able to put one foot in front of the other," (Wright, *Paul for Everyone*, 153).

17. "The way [the gospel] will be 'glorified' among people is by their accepting its message as the good news from God that it really is, and thus themselves becoming followers of the crucified, now glorified, One," (Fee, *Thessalonians*, 314).

18. "The Thessalonians were remarkable examples of the success of the gospel; why not

Given his language, Paul may have had the Isthmian games, hosted in Corinth, in mind. Olympic athletes receive a great deal of honor when they win their respective competitions (cf. Rom 9:16; 1 Cor 9:24; Gal 2:2; 5:7; Phil 2:16). The gold medal, the medal stand, hearing the national anthem, the subsequent applause, adulation, and endorsements—Olympians like track star Michael Johnson or swimming sensation Michael Phelps know what it means to "speed ahead and be honored." In the same way, "God will demonstrate at the end of time that the gospel of Christ is the true 'winner' against all competing worldviews and thus is the only true religion and philosophy."[19]

Paul's second request was to "be delivered from wicked and evil men" (cf. Rom 15:31; 2 Cor 1:8–11). We shouldn't miss the fact that the apostle's desire for safety was secondary to his hope of the gospel's success. If necessary, living and longing for the Lord mandates we eschew personal safety in order to see the gospel break through barriers and overcome opposition. When Christ called us to the gospel, he made clear that it required denial and death (Luke 9:23), so we cannot allege that we were deceived. Nonetheless, the apostle wished for deliverance from wicked and evil men, both Jews and Gentiles (cf. 2 Cor 11:26).

Paul uses a definite article with the phrase "wicked and evil men," so it is thought that he had a particular group/situation in mind, rather than simply speaking in generalities. Life had certainly not been easy for Paul since leaving the city. The Jews had made trouble for him once again in Berea. In Athens, Paul was without the companionship of Silas and Timothy, and the gospel did not receive a very enthusiastic reception there. This brought him to Corinth where he labored for eighteen months, but it too proved to be a difficult ministry. In fact, Luke records that, "When Silas and Timothy arrived from Macedonia, Paul was occupied with the word, testifying to the Jews that the Christ was Jesus. And when they

---

enlist them to pray that the same work of the Spirit be reproduced in Corinth and elsewhere?" (Shogren, *1 & 2 Thessalonians*, 316).

19. Beale, *1–2 Thessalonians*, 237.

opposed and reviled him, he shook out his garments and said to them, 'Your blood be on your own heads! I am innocent. From now on I will go to the Gentiles,'" (Acts 18:5–6).

In the first letter, Paul spoke of evil forces working against him (1 Thess 2:18; 3:5; cf. 1 Cor 16:9). Behind every evil person lies the evil one, but the apostle did not fear Satan because "the Lord is faithful" (cf. Deut 7:9; 32:4; 1 Cor 1:9; 10:13; 2 Cor 1:18; 1 Thess 5:24). He wasn't being naïve about the threats that faced him; this was no feel-good platitude that Paul was clinging to, nor was he burying his head in the sand. He knew "that the really significant factor is the character of his Lord, not the might of the enemy."[20] The same Lord will establish and guard us against Satan[21] (Matt 6:13; 1 John 5:18–19).

Paul concludes with an expression of his confidence in the Thessalonians, confidence that they would obey the directives in the letter. This was a rhetorical way of softening the ground for the difficult conversation he was about to have with them. He needed to discuss the unruly parasites who were refusing to work and negatively affecting the community.[22] Before delving into this topic, however, Paul expresses his gratitude and confidence in the whole congregation and offers a prayer that the Lord would "direct your hearts to the love of God and to the steadfastness of Christ." The apostle knew that, as long as Christians focused on God's love for them and pursued Christ's model of endurance, they would remain stable and persevere until the Lord's return.[23]

---

20. Morris, *Thessalonians*, 248.

21. "To strengthen speaks of the divine work within the believer and is thus subjective; to guard implies the outer working of providence. The Christian may know nothing of it, beyond the bare fact that God is working. From how many evils have we been delivered by the secret mercy of God?" (Ward, *Commentary*, 168–69).

22. "In ancient literature, those in authority at times used the verb 'to have confidence' to express their confidence that their subjects would obey their decrees," (Green, *Thessalonians*, 338).

23. Edwards adds that Paul's prayer was that the Thessalonians would "meditate on God's love to the point where they were motivated to continue to persevere as Christians, despite difficulties and persecutions," (*1 & 2 Thessalonians*, 329).

TALKING POINTS

For the post-apostolic church, "hold to the traditions" means nothing more or less than "hold to Scripture."[24] In the strongest language possible, I must state here that the spiritual health of a congregation is largely dependent on how tightly it clings to Scripture—in practice, not just in theory. Michael Holmes identifies several examples of the church's failure to hold tightly to Scripture: taking verses out of context, claiming to believe the Bible while holding unbiblical beliefs, giving greater weight to secular teaching, emphasizing one part of Scripture to the neglect of another, believing what we want to believe out of convenience, or alleging that Scripture is not relevant to today because circumstances have changed.[25] I have witnessed each of these examples among God's people, and I'm afraid to say that I've been guilty of a few myself. Before church leaders concern themselves with creating a friendly atmosphere, a vibrant youth program, launching an ambitious building campaign, or most anything else, they must consider the prominence they give to Scripture in the life of their congregation. If a church stands firm and holds tightly to Scripture, everything else will fall into place in God's good time.

Paul was not reticent to identify the challenges that faced him and his readers, nor did he allow cognizance of such dangers to paralyze him or hijack his joy and peace. Instead, he subjected all fear and anxiety to the lordship of Christ and declared his trust in Jesus' faithfulness. A word of caution exists here for alarmists who too quickly scream about the sky falling. You know who I'm talking about—those who act as if the cause

---

24. "Today our only access to this apostolic tradition is through what the apostles wrote, specifically, the letters of Paul and others that have become part of the canon of Scripture. Thus, whenever Paul speaks of holding firmly, obeying, receiving, or being taught apostolic *tradition*, we need to think in terms of apostolic *Scripture*. For us today, Scripture is authoritative and normative in the same way that apostolic tradition was for the Thessalonians," (Holmes, *1 and 2 Thessalonians*, 261).

25. Ibid., 265–66.

of Christ in America will be thwarted if you don't forward their email or share/like their (often right-wing) social media status. I'm talking about the peddlers of hate who act as if Islam is lurking at the door, ready to devour all that is good and right in our world, unless you join them in their hate-mongering. Such people pretend that our greatest enemies are Muslims or Democrats or anyone else who is different from us. Wrong! Our enemy is the evil one (Eph 6:12), the one who accuses the church (Rev 12:10). Yet Jesus went all Chuck Norris on the devil on that glorious Easter morning, and the same will happen again on that great day when our King returns in his unparalleled glory to "tread the winepress of the fury of the wrath of God the Almighty" (Rev 19:15). The next time you think everything is going to hell in a hand basket, remember what Paul said to the Thessalonians, then pray this prayer: "Lord, you are faithful. Establish and guard me against the evil one." And then allow him to focus your heart on God's love and Jesus' model of endurance (cf. 1 Pet 2:23).

Having spent a lot of time studying these two letters to Thessalonica, I am both impressed and humbled by the content of the apostle's prayers. It has been an immense privilege to read Paul's petitions, and it strikes me that they sound so different from the prayers we offer up today. After reading many church bulletins, I began to wonder if some among us consider cancer, not Satan, to be our greatest enemy. Shogren points out, "We can assume that the prayer time of Paul's congregations included local needs of health, employment, and so on. Yet, given what we may infer from the letters, it seems that they would have prayed more for missionaries than for, to name one example, the sick."[26] Anyone serious about restoring NT Christianity must restore its priorities in prayer. Like Shogren, I believe in praying for physical needs, but too often, these private prayers become too self-centered. Paul's example beckons us to give priority to praying for stronger leaders, greater holiness, endurance

---

26. Shogren, *1 & 2 Thessalonians,* 319.

in suffering, and the advance of the gospel. If we want to be like the first-century church, we must learn to pray like the first-century church.

10

THE DEVIL'S PLAYGROUND

Among the most pervasive lies Christians easily believe is the notion that work is not holy, but rather a punishment for sin. After all, wasn't Adam cursed with work at the Fall? The answer is a resounding, "No!" Adam was created to work in the garden (Gen 2:15). It was only after the Fall that his work was cursed in that it became difficult, tiresome, and ceased to bring him as much fulfillment as it once did (Gen 3:17–19).

The Bible champions the importance of work. It is not the sum of who we are, but it is nonetheless a vital part of our identity as those created in God's image. Work is a gift from God (Eccl 2:24; 3:13; 5:19–20). One does not have to be a professional preacher or minister to do "the Lord's work," since all work is holy when done to God's glory. Even in heaven, I believe we will perform some type of work in the service of God (Rev 22:3). Therefore, it is no accident that many of Paul's letters contain practical advice about employment, including the relationship between slaves and masters—i.e. workers and employers (e.g. Eph 6:5–7; Col 3:22–4:1).

It was the Puritans who first quipped, "Idle hands are the devil's playground," and Spurgeon once asserted, "There is nothing in the world, next to the grace of God, that is more likely to keep men out of mischief than having plenty to do."[1] The Bible does not condone a life of incessant

1. C. H. Spurgeon, *The Metropolitan Tabernacle Pulpit Sermons*, vol. 51 (London: Passmore, 1905), 168.

busyness. The Sabbath laws of the OT were intended to teach Israel that they needed to take time for God, themselves, and their families, and that the world would not collapse when they did. The NT voided these Sabbath laws, but we do have the example of Christ who took time out to pray to and commune with the Father (Mark 1:35; cf. Ps 46:10).

If the Bible discourages busyness, however, it outright condemns laziness. To varying degrees, we are all attracted to leisure: watching television, surfing the web, snoozing in the hammock, or losing ourselves in a hobby. None of these things are intrinsically wrong, but when enjoying leisure becomes the ultimate goal of living, we have a problem. This applies equally to lazy deadbeats and couch potatoes, but also to those whose mindset is "work hard, then retire and do nothing for the rest of my life."[2] Again, we were created to work so as to bring God glory (John 5:17; 1 Cor 10:31), not sit and twiddle our thumbs in idleness.

In this final section of 2 Thessalonians, Paul addresses lazy idlers in the church. He calls them "unruly" in the sense that they are out of line, but it is clear that he has in mind those who refused to work at all. Such individuals exercised a profound sense of selfishness by insisting that they be allowed to live off the generosity of others—McGarvey labeled the problem "parasitical idleness."[3] They were out of line since they were rejecting the example Paul had set for them when he was in town. Worse, they were bearing a terrible witness to their pagan neighbors who valued a strong work ethic.[4] Paul's words in this passage, therefore, are testimony to just how seriously the Lord considers our work ethic.

This final section also touches on the delicate subject of church

---

2. "Of course retirement can be a vehicle for doing other forms of work and ministry—more time for prayer, more time to do service projects and the like. But it may be doubted that Paul would in any way encourage us to 'save for retirement' or 'look forward to when you don't have to do anything for a living.' He was a man who certainly believed in dying with his boots on," (Witherington, *1 and 2 Thessalonians*, 265).

3. McGarvey, *Thessalonians*, 45.

4. A Roman proverb went something like this: "By doing nothing, men learn to do evil," (Wiersbe, *Be Ready*, 169).

discipline. In our time, church discipline has gone from one extreme to the other. It wasn't that long ago that it was common and even abused in some circles, but today, it is virtually non-existent. Leaders are reluctant to practice it for fear of member revolt or, worse, being castigated by the media.[5] The biblical mandate of church discipline must be restored if we are committed to living for the Lord. As the apostle reminds us in his closing words, souls of beloved brothers and sisters are at stake.

2 THESSALONIANS 3:6-15

Paul once again gives a command in the strongest language possible. This is not a suggestion, but an order, one that carried with it a strong expectation of obedience because the full weight of the authority of the Lord Jesus Christ stood behind this directive.[6] Moreover, "since Christians are those who have called on the name (1 Cor 1:2) of Jesus for salvation, he deserves their absolute obedience as Lord."[7]

The apostle commanded the Thessalonians to "keep away from any brother who is walking in idleness." Two crucial phrases in this sentence need to be properly defined, lest we misunderstand what Paul was saying. The idea behind "keep away" was a nautical one, referring to the furling or rolling up of a sail (Homer, *Odyssey* 3.11, 16.353). It also could mean girding up garments for work (Hesiod, *Shield* 288), a concept not that different from our idiom, "roll up your sleeves." Its metaphorical sense, however, had to do with moving away from someone. Witherington

---

5. In August 2013, a church near Chattanooga, Tennessee withdrew fellowship from a family who approved of their daughter's lesbian lifestyle. The local and national media backlash was brutal. Thanks be to God that the congregation remained firm in their conviction.

6. cf. Matt 10:5; Luke 8:29; 9:21; Acts 1:4; 3:6; 10:42; 16:18; 1 Cor 1:10; 5:3-4; Phil 2:10. "This is at once a reminder of the very real authority that Paul exercised and of the seriousness of any refusal to obey. Paul was not giving some private ideas of his own when he spoke 'in the name,'" (Morris, *Thessalonians*, 252-53).

7. D. Michael Martin, *1, 2 Thessalonians* (Nashville: Broadman, 1995), 272.

suggests "shun" as an appropriate translation (cf. Gal 2:12),[8] but neither the Greek verb nor the context warrants such extreme separation.

Morris argues that the word "stands for the withholding of intimate fellowship. … Such a line of conduct is meant as would impress on the offenders that they had opened up a gap between themselves and the rest. They had to be made to see that complete fellowship is possible only when there is complete harmony."[9] Notice that Morris essentially argues for cessation of *intimate* fellowship, not total disassociation. This interpretation is strengthened by Paul's later words, "Do not regard him as an enemy, but warn him as a brother" (3:15). What he has in mind, then, is not a withdrawal of fellowship per se, but a scaling back of fellowship. Remember, when they furled the sails, they didn't remove them all together.

Paul's warning against those "walking in idleness" must also be properly understood. First, his comments seem restricted to fellow Christians (i.e. "any brother"). However we interpret "walking in idleness," we should realize that it does not apply to those of the world. This is a critical distinction.

Second, whom does Paul mean when he refers to those "walking in idleness"? As we saw in 1 Thess 5:14, the root Greek verb literally meant "to be out of order," i.e. out of line. The word was used in Greek literature (e.g. Xenophon, *Cyropaedia* 7.2.6) for military desertion and lack of discipline. Thucydides used the term to describe the Peloponnesians retreating in a disorderly way back to their camp after being defeated in battle (*Histories* 3.108). Paul likely has in mind the same "idle" or unruly persons he mentioned in the previous letter.[10] In this passage, he has in mind those unwilling to work, though the apostle does not use the conventional Greek words that mean "lazy." He instead preferred a term

---

8. "Shunning is intended to make clear to the disorderly brother that his behavior is inappropriate and unacceptable," (Witherington, *1 and 2 Thessalonians*, 250).

9. Morris, *Thessalonians*, 253.

10. Shogren argues with Bible versions that render *ataktoi* as "lazy"—"These translators are making the text say more than it really does," (*1 & 2 Thessalonians*, 325).

that carried with it the accusation of acting contrary to God's will and the apostle's instruction and example.[11]

Fee observes, "It is not 'idleness' per se that concerns Paul, but the unruly nature of their refusal to work and thus disrupting the *shalom* of the entire community that concerns him. Against that kind of 'idleness' there should be much legitimate concern in any community of faith."[12] I completely agree that the idle were disrupting the peace and unity of the body, but Fee goes one step too far when he suggests that idleness itself was not Paul's concern. We were created to work and perpetual idleness spurns God's will for us.

Third, I have a hard time believing the problem at hand existed at Thessalonica because some believed in the imminent return of Christ. Nowhere does Paul explicitly connect the two. Nothing in the text expressly says these idle persons had quit their jobs because they thought the end was near. In those passages where Paul discusses the Second Coming, he never mentions the idle of Thessalonica.[13] On the other hand, it has been argued that the problem was rooted in the first-century social phenomenon known as the patron-client relationship.

> In this relationship, members of the lower class attached themselves to benefactors from among the upper class, from whom they then received sustenance and help in various matters in exchange for the obligation to reciprocate with expressions of gratitude and support. It is argued that Paul's converts included those of the urban poor who had formed client relationships with wealthy

---

11. "The primary emphasis is not on their lazy character but rather their unwillingness to conform to the apostolic rule," (Green, *Thessalonians*, 343, n. 28; cf. Malherbe, *Thessalonians*, 450).

12. Fee, *Thessalonians*, 335.

13. "The great body of commentators, including the ablest, attribute this idleness to the erroneous notion that the Lord was about to come; but there is no hint of this in the text," (McGarvey, *Thessalonians*, 47; cf. Malherbe, *Thessalonians*, 253; B. N. Kaye, "Eschatology and Ethics in 1 and 2 Thessalonians," *NovT* 17 [1975]: 47–57).

members in the Thessalonian church, but who exploited
the generosity of their new Christian patrons.[14]

In other words, some members of the first-century Thessalonian
church wanted to live off the largesse of others. Marshall argues for another
view, that idleness was due to the prevailing attitude in first-century Greek
culture towards manual labor,[15] although R. Russell contends this was an
attitude mainly held by the wealthy, and that the Thessalonian Christians
were typically from the poorer classes.[16] Whatever the exact situation,
Paul was deeply concerned that some Christians did not have a God-
honoring work ethic and thus were not living for the Lord as they should.

Teaching followers by example (3:9) was an established practice among
first-century philosophers. A personal example was preferred "because they
were regarded as more persuasive than words and as providing concrete
models to imitate."[17] If you detect in this passage a level of exasperation on
Paul's part, it's because the apostle knew these unruly folks were not living
consistently with the pattern he had so painstakingly set for them. It was
his prerogative to be supported financially by the Thessalonians as he
ministered among them, but Paul had chosen not to exercise that right. He
instead supported himself by making tents (Acts 18:3). As John MacArthur
points out, they may have stayed in Jason's house (Acts 17:7), but Paul
and his companions paid their own way.[18] In addition, Paul resented the
insinuation that he or any other godly leader was "in it for the money" (Acts
20:33–35; 1 Tim 3:3; Tit 1:7; cf. 1 Sam 12:3–5; Heb 13:5; 1 Pet 5:2).

---

14. ZIBBC 3:439.

15. Marshall, *1 and 2 Thessalonians*, 223; cf. Leland Ryken, *Work & Leisure in the Christian Perspective* (Portland, OR: Multnomah, 1987), 64–65.

16. R. Russell, "The Idle in 2 Thess 3.6–12: An Eschatological or a Social Problem?" *NTS* 34 (1988): 105–19.

17. Abraham J. Malherbe, *Moral Exhortation, a Greco-Roman Sourcebook* (Philadelphia: Westminster Press, 1986), 135.

18. MacArthur, *1 & 2 Thessalonians*, 306.

In addition to his strong example, Paul also reminds his readers of the command he had given: "If anyone is not willing[19] to work, let him not eat." Adolf Deissmann suggested Paul was borrowing a common, blue-collar proverb from the workshop,[20] but such a work ethic seems to have been widely held in Judaism. Commenting on Gen 1:2, Rabbi Abbahu said, "If I do not work, I do not eat," (Genesis Rabbah 2.2; cf. Philo, *On Abraham* 20–21). In fact, Scripture itself places a high premium on the importance of work (Gen 3:17–19; Ps 128:2; Prov 10:4; 12:11; 19:15; Eph 4:28; 1 Thess 4:11–12). In chapter 12, the author of the Didache warned:

> Everyone "who comes in the name of the Lord" is to be welcomed. But then examine him, and you will find out— for you will have insight—what is true and what is false. If the one who comes is merely passing through, assist him as much as you can. But he must not stay with you for more than two or, if necessary, three days. However, if he wishes to settle among you and is a craftsman, let him work for his living. But if he is not a craftsman, decide according to your own judgment how he shall live among you as a Christian, yet without being idle. But if he does not wish to cooperate in this way, then he is trading on Christ. Beware of such people.

Having reminded the Thessalonians of his command, Paul then echoed the advice he gave in 1 Thess 4:11–12. This time, however, he employs a play on words to get his point across: "They are not busy; they are busybodies" (2 Thess 3:11 NIV). In other words, they are

---

19. "Paul is not speaking of those who cannot find work, nor of those who through injury or illness are not able to work, but of those who deliberately choose not to work," (Morris, *Thessalonians*, 256, n. 22).

20. Adolf Deissmann, *Light from the Ancient Near East*, trans. Lionel R. M. Strachan (Grand Rapids: Baker, 1978), 314.

"hardly working" instead of "working hard."[21] To avoid the possibility of misunderstanding, Paul again uses emphatic language—"Such persons we command and encourage in the Lord Jesus Christ to do their work quietly and to earn their own living" (3:12). Wanamaker captures the sternness and solemnity of these words: "The command has coercive power: to reject it is to reject the Lord Jesus Christ himself and therefore to exclude oneself from the community."[22] Bruce believes Paul's words are meant to do more than invoke Christ's lordship and authority; they "may imply Christ's personal involvement in the situation."[23] If this is the case, it emphasizes how important our work ethic is to the Lord.

Paul also gives a further command concerning those who might reject his letter (and, by extension, the call to obedience/work and abandonment of idleness). "If anyone does not obey what we say in this letter, take note of that person, and have nothing to do with him, that he may be ashamed" (3:14). The Greek verb translated "take note" occurs here and nowhere else in the NT, although Paul says something very similar in Rom 16:17—"Watch out for those who cause divisions and create obstacles contrary to the doctrine that you have been taught; avoid them." He also commands the Thessalonians to disassociate from that person (cf. 1 Cor 5:9, 11), which may have given rise to what later was termed "excommunication."[24] He does not have in mind total shunning in the sense of refusing to acknowledge someone's existence, but a scaling back of fellowship so as to make clear that things are not all right. It's important that we not lose sight of Paul's goal for this discipline. "Warn him as a brother" makes clear that the apostle sought restoration. As Ward reminds us, "Unbrotherly criticism may do more harm than good."[25] Therefore, any discipline imposed by churches today must seek the same

---

21. Holmes, *1 and 2 Thessalonians*, 273.

22. Wanamaker, *Thessalonians*, 287.

23. Bruce, *1 & 2 Thessalonians*, 207.

24. Holmes, *1 and 2 Thessalonians*, 275.

25. Ward, *Commentary*, 172.

result as Paul's recommendation.

The apostle then gives a friendly caution that the Thessalonians in good standing not allow[26] the unruly to rob them of their kindness (3:13). The verb he used meant to "lose enthusiasm, be discouraged,"[27] (cf. Gal 6:9). John Calvin lamented:

> It is usually the case that those who are often generous withdraw their help when they see their aid is not beneficial. Here we have a statement that is worthy of particular note—no matter how ungrateful, morose, proud, arrogant some poor people may be, no matter how much they annoy and irritate us, we must nevertheless never stop trying to be of assistance to them.[28]

Ungrateful, lazy leeches on the community can eventually rob everyone of their motivation for generosity. We must remember, however, that although some abuse "the system," we should not stop meeting the needs of others.[29] Consider the Psalms: "Blessed is the one who considers the poor!" (Ps 41:1); "The righteous is generous and gives" (Ps 37:21). Solomon warned, "Those who give to the poor will lack nothing, but those who close their eyes to them receive many curses" (Prov 28:27 NIV). In

---

26. Malherbe notes that the injunction in the Greek is in the aorist subjunctive, meaning the Thessalonians had not yet grown weary, and that Paul was exhorting them not "to stop doing good altogether," (*Thessalonians*, 458).

27. BDAG 272.

28. Calvin, *1, 2 Thessalonians*, 107–8.

29. Fee makes an intriguing point based on Paul's words here: "One should also note how Pauline this emphasis is. It is common in several contemporary situations, where Paul is considered as something of a theological hero, to think in terms of 'doing the *right* thing.' Although such language is not totally foreign to the apostle, his own emphasis is usually to be found in the present language, 'doing what is *good*.' This may seem like a small matter to some; but it is an unfortunate part of church history that God's people are far more often concerned about the 'right thing' than 'the good thing,' and often in ways that abandon altogether what is good. While Paul is concerned about both, his own emphases tend to lie with the latter, as in the present passage. After all, it is the 'good thing' that is most often also the 'right thing,'" (*Thessalonians*, 336–37).

our own church culture, I know how easy it is to become disenchanted with helping the poor, given the high rate of exploitation. Christ-like compassion, however, demands we always be eager to help "the least of these," no matter the likelihood of our being cheated or abused. To do otherwise is to run the grave risk of losing our enthusiasm and will to do good to all those created in the image of God.

2 THESSALONIANS 3:16–18

Paul's benediction at the end of this letter returns to a prominent theme of both epistles: peace.[30] He wishes for his readers "peace at all times in every way," acknowledging that such can only come from the Lord Jesus Christ[31] (cf. Num 6:26; Rom 15:33). Paul's wish for the Thessalonians is Christ's wish for all his churches at all times. This is why Spurgeon concluded, "What a sweet benediction! And how he heaps the words together, as if peace was one of the greatest blessings a church could have."[32] Christians can be at peace with one another in the midst of difficult circumstances because of Christ's presence (Rom 5:1). Peace is not found in the elimination of all conflict, but in constant communion with Jesus.

Paul, at the very end of the letter, appears to have taken the pen from his amanuensis and signed a brief postscript.[33] "I, Paul, write this greeting with my own hand. This is the sign of genuineness in every letter of mine; it

---

30. "This request for peace fittingly looks back to the two major concerns of the letter: the anxiety within the Thessalonian church over the claim that the day of the Lord had already come and the internal tensions due to the problem of the idlers," (CNTUOT 888).

31. "Thus once more, again in an especially significant way, Paul has appropriated what strictly belonged to Yahweh in an Old Testament passage and applied it directly to Christ," (Fee, *Thessalonians*, 341).

32. C. H. Spurgeon, *The Metropolitan Tabernacle Pulpit Sermons*, vol. 51 (London: Passmore, 1905), 168.

33. "There is abundant evidence, both in the papyri and in the epistolary literature, that letters frequently exhibited two hands: the body is written in the first hand, and the signature, or some more elaborate postscriptum to the body, is written in the second hand," (Gordon J. Bahr, "The Subscriptions in the Pauline Letters," *JBL* 87 [1968]: 32; cf. Morris, *Thessalonians*, 263–64).

is the way I write" (3:17). Such a statement is not uncommon in his letters (cf. 1 Cor 16:21; Gal 6:11; Col 4:18; Phlm 19), nor was it uncommon for other authors of antiquity.[34] Some wrote their own letters, but it was just as often that a secretary, known as an amanuensis, copied down the letter dictated to them by the author. Paul also used the skills of an amanuensis in this way (e.g. Tertius, Rom 16:22). Several ancient letters that have survived to modern times show a change of handwriting where the author signed his name.[35] "Since the change of script would have been obvious to the reader of the letter, there was no reason to state explicitly that the author was now writing rather than the secretary."[36] The apostle does so here to draw attention to the authenticity of the letter, an important factor given his concern over a previous bogus letter (2 Thess 2:2).

Paul finishes his correspondence with the benediction, "The grace of our Lord Jesus Christ be with you all." I may be reading too much into the statement, but perhaps Paul added the word "all" as a signal to the unruly at Thessalonica.[37] He wished for all the saints to experience and abide in Jesus' grace, even those who were at the same time rejecting Jesus' lordship.

34. e.g. Cicero, *To Atticus* 7.3, 12; 8.1; 13.28; cf. Stanley K. Stowers, *Letter Writing in Greco-Roman Antiquity* (Philadelphia: Westminster Press, 1986).

35. For one such example, see Everett Ferguson, *Backgrounds of Early Christianity*, 2nd ed. (Grand Rapids: Eerdmans, 1993), 121.

36. ZIBBC 3:441.

37. Wanamaker, *Thessalonians*, 293.

TALKING POINTS

R ecent statistics reveal that the average American's attitude towards the workplace is less than positive. About 70% claim that they hate their job,[38] and other studies indicate that men are 20% more likely to have a heart attack on Monday morning (15% for women) than any other day of the week.[39] That some would rather die than go to work after the weekend puts a whole new meaning on the phrase "case of the Mondays." What is a biblical, balanced view of work? Obviously, some choose not to work, preferring to mooch off of government welfare instead. It is just as ungodly, however, to have an attitude that considers work as a means to an end, whether that end is peer recognition, material wealth, or hedonistic pleasure. A biblical and balanced view will perceive work as a necessary component of living for the Lord. Work provides more than food and shelter for our families; God uses work, in part, to give us a sense of fulfillment in life. The drive to master a skill, to be the best in our field, is a reflection of the image of God in us. While it is certainly not wrong to retire from full-time employment, it is a terrible distortion of the truth to ever think that we can retire from serving God and those around us.

I n his comments on this passage, N. T. Wright observes, "Most modern Western churches hate the idea of discipline; it seems so 'unloving'. Of course there is such a thing as harsh or self-serving discipline. But if there is a genuine problem the sooner it is dealt with the better. Otherwise one is actually being unloving to everybody else."[40] Every congregation must struggle with the apparent paradox of withdrawing from the unruly while still treating them as brothers. Morris points out, "Our difficulty in combining the two thoughts of withdrawing fellowship and treating the

---

38. Kelli B. Grant, "Americans hate their jobs, even with perks," *USA Today,* June 30, 2013.

39. Anahad O'Connor, "The Claim: Heart Attacks Are More Common on Mondays," *New York Times,* March 14, 2006.

40. Wright, *Paul for Everyone,* 157.

person as a brother should not blind us to the fact that Paul expected the church to be capable of both at once. Neither could be neglected."[41] It would be arrogant and presumptuous of me to pretend that I'm the wise old sage in this matter. Passages such as Matt 18; Rom 16:17–18; 1 Cor 5; Tit 3:9–11 must be considered along with this one. Important questions should be asked, such as: how private/public was the sin? Are there various degrees of withdrawal of fellowship? Also, before any discipline is exercised, leaders should ask if kindness is the prevailing attitude (cf. Rom 2:4) rather than a vindictive desire to humiliate. If there is reluctance to discipline, could it spring from a distorted, perverted form of love? Sometimes it is actually discipline that proves to be the loving thing to do (Heb 12:6). It must be stated, and in the strongest terms, that a desire to please God should trump any fear of fallout. Finally, this heavy subject should inspire all Christians to pray for their leaders since they are tasked with discerning wisdom in these volatile situations.[42]

It must be restated in the strongest terms that this passage does not apply to non-Christians. It is shameful for any congregation or Christian to appeal to this passage as an excuse *not* to help the needy. Perhaps some of us need to hear again Paul's order not to "grow weary in doing good." "What could be more Christlike than persisting in well-doing even when the beneficiaries of love in action do not deserve or appreciate the sacrifice made on their behalf?"[43] The county where I minister has a large number of low-income families and is also purported to be the crystal-meth capital of Texas, so it is understandable that we receive numerous benevolence requests. I confess that it's easy to become calloused to the never-ending stream of people looking for a handout but with no interest in spiritual things. I don't believe the church should be

41. Morris, *Thessalonians*, 260–61.

42. I highly recommend reading Michael E. Phillips, "Creative Church Discipline," *Leadership* 7, no. 4 (1986): 46–50.

43. Martin, *1, 2 Thessalonians*, 285.

the community piggy bank, but I do believe that benevolence should be a budget priority—repaving the parking lot or installing a new kitchen in the fellowship hall can wait. Perhaps the process for getting help should also be simplified in some cases; if a person can get a U.S. passport easier than they can receive assistance from your congregation, it's time to streamline. In the end, the church should always strive to go above and beyond in helping "the least of these." As the world violently shoves the church to the margins, we maintain a significant measure of our cultural relevancy by being generous to those who don't always appreciate it. It is, after all, the example Jesus set for us (Luke 23:34; Rom 5:8), and when he returns, he will ask how generous we were to "the least of these" (Matt 25:31–46). As we live and long for the Lord, let us not neglect those who need him most.

ABBREVIATIONS

BDAG	*A Greek-English Lexicon of the New Testament and Other Early Christian Literature.* 3rd ed. Chicago: Univ. of Chicago Press, 2000.
BBR	*Bulletin of Biblical Research*
CBQ	*Catholic Biblical Quarterly*
CNTUOT	*Commentary on the New Testament Use of the Old Testament.* Ed., G. K. Beale and D. A. Carson. Grand Rapids: Baker, 2007.
ESV	English Standard Version
ExpTim	*Expository Times*
HCSB	Holman Christian Study Bible
HTR	*Harvard Theological Review*
KJV	King James Version
JBL	*Journal of Biblical Literature*
JETS	*Journal of the Evangelical Theological Society*
JSNT	*Journal for the Study of the New Testament*
JTS	*Journal of Theological Studies*
LXX	Septuagint, the Greek translation of the Old Testament
Msg	The Message

NASU	New American Standard Bible — Updated Edition
NCV	New Century Version
NIDDNTT	*New International Dictionary of New Testament Theology.* 5 vols. Ed. Colin Brown. Grand Rapids: Zondervan, 1986.
NIV	New International Version
NKJV	New King James Version
NLT	New Living Translation
NovT	*Novum Testamentum*
NRSV	New Revised Standard Version
NTS	*New Testament Studies*
NT	New Testament
OT	Old Testament
TDNT	*Theological Dictionary of the New Testament.* 10 vols. Ed., Gerhard Kittel, Gerhard, Geoffrey W. Bromiley, and Gerhard Friedrich. Grand Rapids: Eerdmans, 1964–76.
TynBul	*Tyndale Bulletin*
ZIBBC	*Zondervan Illustrated Bible Backgrounds Commentary.* 4 vols. Ed. Clinton E. Arnold. Grand Rapids: Zondervan, 2002.

ACKNOWLEDGMENTS

I must first express my gratitude for the ministry and writings of John William McGarvey (1829–1911). My eyes were initially opened to the treasures of these epistles by his commentary on the Thessalonian correspondence.

To God's gift of coffee and M&Ms—my performance-enhancing drugs. They keep me fueled during my marathon research/writing sessions.

To my church family in Bowie for the incredible support you have given me. I am confident that Paul, too, would boast of you in all the churches of God (2 Thess 1:4). You are my glory, joy, and crown (1 Thess 2:19–20).

To Brandon Edwards, Ethan Garrett, and others who so graciously supported this project with their prayers and generosity. Your support made a tremendous difference.

To my many friends who read portions of the manuscript and offered terrific feedback. To Sheri Glazier, Rebecca Thompson, and Jena Webb for great editorial work.

To Dr. Earl Edwards. Thank you for lending your endorsement to this project and for being so gracious with such a tight deadline.

To Jesse Robertson for requiring me to read through the NT books during the spring semester of my junior year of college. May we all give ourselves to the public reading of Scripture to the glory of its Author.

To Shirley Eaton. Had I known the tremendous help you would later give me, this grateful Hittite would have stayed behind that summer to help transition from Dewey to LOC.

To my long-suffering wife. The way you lovingly nurture our son inspires me to, like Paul, nurture God's saints. I love you.

To my son. Words cannot express the joy God has brought to our lives by entrusting you to us. You make me smile every day.

To my dad. Because you lived and longed for the Lord, I don't grieve as one without hope.

To the Lord Jesus Christ. Your church eagerly anticipates the day when you will be glorified in us, and we in you. Come quickly, merciful Savior.

BIBLIOGRAPHY

Barclay, William. *The Letters to the Philippians, Colossians, and Thessalonians*. Rev. ed. Philadelphia: Westminster Press, 1975.

Beale, G. K. *1-2 Thessalonians*. Downers Grove, IL: InterVarsity Press, 2003.

Best, Ernest. *A Commentary on the First and Second Epistles to the Thessalonians*. Peabody, MA: Hendrickson, 1988.

Bruce, F. F. *1 & 2 Thessalonians*. Dallas: Word, 1982.

Calvin, John. *1, 2 Thessalonians*. Wheaton, IL: Crossway, 1999.

Coffman, James Burton. *Commentary on 1 & 2 Thessalonians, 1 & 2 Timothy, Titus & Philemon*. Austin: Firm Foundation, 1978.

Comfort, Philip W. "1 & 2 Thessalonians" in *Cornerstone Biblical Commentary*. Vol. 16. Carol Stream, IL: Tyndale House, 2008.

Demarest, Gary W. *1, 2 Thessalonians, 1, 2 Timothy, Titus*. Waco: Word, 1984.

Edwards, Earl D. *1 & 2 Thessalonians*. Searcy, AR: Resource Publications, 2008.

Fee, Gordon D. *The First and Second Letters to the Thessalonians*. Grand Rapids: Eerdmans, 2009.

Gaventa, Beverly Roberts. *First and Second Thessalonians*. Louisville: John Knox, 1998.

Green, Gene L. *The Letters to the Thessalonians*. Grand Rapids: Eerdmans, 2002.

Henry, Matthew. *Commentary on the Whole Bible*. Vol. 6. New York: Revell, 1935.

Holmes, Michael W. *1 and 2 Thessalonians*. Grand Rapids: Zondervan, 1998.

Jackman, David. *The Authentic Church*. Ross-shire, Great Britain: Christian Focus, 1998.

Kaiser, Walter C., Jr. *Hard Sayings of the Bible*. Downers Grove, IL: InterVarsity Press, 1996.

Keener, Craig S. *The IVP Bible Background Commentary: New Testament*. Downers Grove: InterVarsity Press, 1993.

Kelcy, Raymond C. *The Letters of Paul to the Thessalonians*. Austin: Sweet, 1968.

Lightfoot, J. B. *Notes on the Epistles of St. Paul*. London: Macmillan, 1895.

Lipscomb, David. *A Commentary on the New Testament Epistles*. Vol. 5. Ed. J. W. Shepherd. Nashville: Gospel Advocate, 1983.

MacArthur, John. *1 & 2 Thessalonians*. Chicago: Moody Press, 2002.

Maclaren, Alexander. *Expositions of Holy Scripture: Philippians, Colossians, First and Second Thessalonians and First Timothy*. Grand Rapids: Baker, 1978.

Malherbe, Abraham J. *The Letters to the Thessalonians*. New York: Doubleday, 2000.

Marshall, I. Howard. *1 and 2 Thessalonians*. Grand Rapids: Eerdmans, 1983.

Martin, D. Michael. *1, 2 Thessalonians*. Nashville: Broadman, 1995.

McGarvey, J. W., and Philip Y. Pendleton. *Thessalonians, Corinthians, Galatians and Romans*. Cincinnati: Standard Publishing, 1916.

Metzger, Bruce M. *A Textual Commentary on the Greek New Testament*. 2nd ed. Stuttgart: German Bible Society, 1994.

Morris, Leon. *The First and Second Epistles to the Thessalonians*. Rev. ed.

Grand Rapids: Eerdmans, 1991.

Shogren, Gary. *1 & 2 Thessalonians*. Grand Rapids: Zondervan, 2012.

Stott, John. *The Message of Thessalonians*. Downers Grove, IL: InterVarsity Press, 1991.

Wanamaker, Charles A. *The Epistles to the Thessalonians*. Grand Rapids: Eerdmans, 1990.

Ward, Ronald A. *Commentary on 1 & 2 Thessalonians*. Waco: Word, 1973.

Whiteley, D. E. H. *Thessalonians*. London: Oxford Univ. Press, 1969.

Wiersbe, Warren W. *Be Ready*. Wheaton, IL: Victor Books, 1979.

Witherington, Ben, III. *1 and 2 Thessalonians*. Grand Rapids: Eerdmans, 2006.

Woodson, William. *Perfecting Faith*. Brentwood, TN: Penmann Books, 2000.

Wright, Tom. *Paul for Everyone: Galatians and Thessalonians*. Louisville: Westminster John Knox, 2004.

ὥσπερ ξένοι χαίρουσι πατρίδα βλέπειν
οὕτως καὶ τοῖς κάμνουσι βιβλίου τέλος

61846901R00109

Made in the USA
Lexington, KY
22 March 2017